Jim Yocom

Go ahead, peek inside

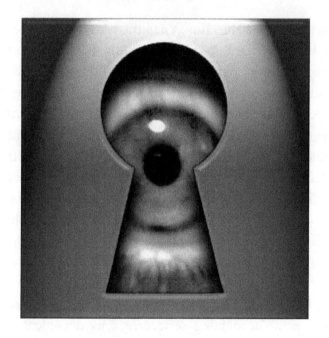

Earnings Disclaimer: Do not buy this product if you think it will automatically make you money just because you bought it. The results shown in this book aren't typical and your results could be more or less than those shown. I will do everything I can to help you make money but in the end it's up to you.

SPECIAL NOTICE

Throughout this book there are many screen shots of various county websites. Of course these are screen shots of the county sites as they existed at the time the book was being written.

Counties constantly change, and generally improve their websites. A website can look one way today and can be changed by an upgrade the very next day. It is impossible to keep every screen shot up to date at all times.

I have never found an instance where you can't find the same information in the update as existed previously. It just may be in a different format. So don't be upset. The information is rarely changed, it is just presented differently.

Jim Yocom

For my wife Barb, who steadfastly supplies the wind beneath my wings. I could never have finished this book without her faith in me when I needed it most.

Also thanks to our grandchildren Kevin, Eric, Matt, Lauren and Aaron for the use of their names which I attached to the characters you are about to meet.

TABLE OF CONTENTS

*Read everything, but especially check out chapters marked with *

Forward

Here you will meet four close friends and learn how a water seeking golf ball starts a conversation that changes all their lives

Introduction

Meet the Honda POS and the Cadillac that replaced it

Chapter 1 - *At the 19th Hole*

Kevin introduces his friends to a whole new world of 36% to 108% rates of interest and piques their curiosity with tales of $50,000 real estate for $25

Chapter 2 - *The View From 30,000 Feet*

The friends meet Lauren who warns them to believe nothing she says, then proceeds to tell them a brown bag lunch and pop from the fridge creates $1,286 in monthly income FOR LIFE – go figure

Chapter 3 - *Here Is Where It Starts*

Here is where they find the vault containing all those high interest rate deals and how real estate values can drop over 60% and their investments are still secured 37 to 1

Chapter 4 - *The Protégés Learn More Than One Way*

They choose their own beginning interest rates; from 8% to 36%, all guaranteed by the government – REALLY

Chapter 5 - *Peek Behind The Curtain*

Like Shopping for guaranteed interest rates at Wal-Mart

Chapter 6 - *How To Beat The Pants Off The Best Wall Street Guru And Never Get Off Your Couch*

Kevin shows the protégés how he invested $954,825.82 in one day from his couch

Chapter 7 - *Okay, So You Want Some Property*

Everything is bigger in Texas. The protégés learn how to earn 300% in Texas

Chapter 8 - *Kevin Drops A Bomb*

Here is where the protégés actually learn how to buy $50,000+ chunks of real estate for just $25 – sometimes less, with Kevin's magic letter

Chapter 9 - *Kevin Puts The Program On Steroids*

How to sell the property before you even own it. You will own it for a few minutes though.

**Chapter 10 - *The Pay Window Is Open*

Kevin introduces them to a unique bank and gives them the address. Here is the bank's recent ad:

Need a new car?

Let Our Bank Finance It For You

- No Down Payment

- We Don't Even Check Your Credit

- Free and Clear Title.....Immediately

- We Pay **YOU** Double Digit Interest On Each Monthly Payment

- When You Finish All Your Monthly Payments, Drop By The Bank And We Will Give All Your Money Back – And A Profit

- Here's An Example: Car Sells For $20,000. Finance For 48 Months At $488 Per Month....Total Payments Equal $23,424. At End Of 48 Months Come By The Bank And Tells Us What To Do. Here Are Your Options

- We Can Give You A Check For $35,444

- We Can Pay You $472 Per Month – FOREVER

- Or Just Leave The $35,444 In The Bank And It Will Grow To $689,767 In 20 Years And Provide $9,196 Per Month In Income FOREVER.......It's Your Choice

Chapter 11 - *Of Course You Can Collect Interest On Your Car Payments....... Oh Yes You Can*

Protégés meet the owner of the bank and learn how he pays them 16% interest on their car payments. Simple when you know how

Chapter 12 - *You Can Deduct Your Kids Sneakers, Video Games, Concert Tickets And Mileage When You Drive Them To School. Oh Yes You Can*

Pay out of one pocket – not deductible. Pay from the other pocket and they are all deductible.

Chapter 13 - *There are two tax systems. You can choose which is best for you.*

Your choice can change your whole life.

Chapter 14 - *It is time to get serious about your money*

How you do anything, is how you do everything. Time to apply what they have learned.

Chapter 15 - *The complete Synergy System*

"Whatever you can do, or dream you can, begin it. Boldness has genius power and magic in it." Goethe

FORWARD

Authors write books for many different reasons. Some have imagined a story they want to share. Some want to teach. Some want to tell all about themselves. Probably most authors have a bit of each that motivates them.

I am no different, in most ways, although I am not compelled to write my life story. Nor have I imagined another "<u>Atlas Shrugged</u>," or "<u>Gone With The Wind</u>." My motivation is to sound a warning. I am not going to spend a lot of time on the warning. You just have to watch the news, or read a newspaper, then spend five minutes thinking about what you have heard about where the world is now. You will come to the conclusion, on your own, that it is possible for a lot of bad things to happen to us in the days ahead.

That's enough warning. If you don't get it on your own, no amount of words I could share with you will turn on your warning light.

Years ago, more years than I am willing to admit publicly, when I was suffering major brain damage in corporate America, I had a standing rule for all of my direct reports; Never bring me a problem until you have come up with a solution. I might not use their solution, but I wanted them to invest enough brain power to at least have a solution

I still live by that rule. I have pointed you to a major problem, so it is incumbent on me to offer my solution. You must take charge of your own future and in the following pages I am laying out details of my solution.

I have written several books in the past. They have all been instructional and this one is only different in the presentation. I am presenting it in story form, something I haven't done. Hopefully, I have not let the story get in the way of the instruction.

This story has several facets. The storyline itself is mostly fictional but the story is based on autobiographical events in the lives of the author and his lovely wife, Barb. The techniques, strategies, real estate and Tax Lien Certificate information, home based business opportunities etc. are totally factual. You are furnished links to check out everything for yourself as you progress through the book.

Some events are based on incidents that happened to other people; who are in one way or another involved with the author. The Lauren in our story is a composite of different mentors, coaches and advisors to the author in real life. However this book itself will serve you well as your surrogate Lauren.

Jim Yocom, Author

This is the story of four close friends. They are very much alike in many ways, and couldn't be more different in others. Maybe the differences are why they are friends. They have different incomes, different educations, and different careers.

Three of the four share the common goals of providing better incomes for their families and more secure futures. The economy has them as worried as the rest of America.

The fourth friend stands out from the other three. He is older than his companions and is now very wealthy. It was not always so. He and his wife were as far under water as the golf ball you are about to meet. His wealth has not changed him though, and he is still very close to the other three.

They have all known each other for a few years and the three have watched this fourth member as his fortunes have varied from modest success, to what appeared to everyone to be an economic disaster. Then they watched in almost open mouth wonder as his fortunes seemed to change overnight.

They never asked how he created his wealth and he never talked about it.

That is about to change. This is the story of this rich man, how he got so rich, the lady who played a major role in his rise to riches and *The Secret Synergy Group System.*

You will learn, step by step, how he created his wealth and how you can do the same by just following the exact steps the lady laid out for him. If you take the same steps, you can expect the same results as surely as the sun will rise in the East.

Some words of caution – You must really want the wealth. It doesn't matter where you start. The fourth friend started his road to wealth with only two assets:

1. His accumulated knowledge

2. His friendship with the lady who showed him how to put his own life together

You will learn what he knows and this book will serve you as well as the lady served him.

I had originally intended to release this book later this year; in the fall, probably. But it seems to me that things are happening so fast that we all need to act quickly to get our house in order and take control of our future.

I think we have an obligation to learn as much as we can, then pass it on to our children, our grandchildren and anyone who will listen.

If nothing else, recent events have certainly shown us that we can't rely on the government, or even company sponsored plans. This book will not teach you how, nor advise you to turn your hard earned money over to some so called, "Expert." If they are so good at managing money, how do they find time away from their own investments to manage someone else's?

Hhmmm!

Jim Yocom

"...though no one can go back and make a brand new start --
anyone can start right now and make a brand new ending..."

- Anonymous

THE SECRET SYNERGY GROUP SYSTEM

INTRODUCTION

"Dadgummit, there goes another one in the water."

"It looks like your golf ball is under about the same amount of water as my 401k and the equity in my home. I don't seem to be able to get them above water either." Matt grumbled.

Eric had just hit his third shot of the day into a water hazard. Matt wasn't playing any better. It was obvious that something was bothering him. The money comments made it clear what was on his mind.

Eric Taylor, Matt Ryan, Kevin Daniels and Aaron Michaels are taking a rare break in the middle of the week. The four of them make up the Fund Raising Committee of the West Hills Lion's Club. They are planning the various fund raising programs for the coming year and used that as an excuse to take an afternoon off from work.

"Is your 401k account still in the tank? Your company seems to be improving. Isn't your plan doing better too?" Kevin asked. He was genuinely concerned for his friend.

Matt works for a telecommunication company that had been a darling of Wall Street until a couple of years ago. He had been fortunate to survive several rounds of downsizing but never knew if he might be included in the next round of layoffs.

"Actually I guess I am better off than some. Most of the people in the company had all their funds invested in the company's stock. The Chapter 11 reorganization wiped that out totally. I had eighty percent in company stock and twenty percent in a money market account. Of course my eighty percent stock portion is gone for good but I still have what was in the money market account. I only lost eighty percent of my investment. My money market fund is paying less than 2%, but that is better than a total loss.

"But it is more than that. All my life I have worked hard to support my family, but that just isn't enough. I'm like Alice in Wonderland; I run as fast as I can just to stand in one place. We are in debt and we struggle just to survive week to week.

"I really want Malone and the kids to have the life we dreamed of building. I really love them and it hurts not to give them the good lifestyle I had always planned.

"Malone works just to give us some extra money. We never planned on her doing that.

"I need that magic genie from *The Secret* to take me by the hand and show me how to increase my income. I'm not asking for someone to do it for me. I just want to find the 'how' and have a bit of backup when I need it.

"Sorry to go on like this, I am just so frustrated. The worst part is that I don't see an end to it."

Eric had been listening carefully to Matt and nodding his head. "I know just how you feel. I have been working for almost twenty years building my retirement and assets to provide a good education for the kids, and for Allison and me to travel around the country. But this lousy economy has knocked the value of my business down by almost 30% and the real estate that we were going to sell to fund part of our retirement is now worth less than what I owe. So Matt save one of the genie's wishes for me.

"I am sorry to be blowing off steam with you, Kevin. I have been looking for other things that I can do but there is just so much junk out there that promises to make you rich in 90 days. We know that isn't going to happen. But I really need a plan so I can actually have control of my future. What I've done so far is not going to get me where my family needs to be."

"Maybe I'm lucky to work for a small company that doesn't have a company plan," Aaron said. "I used to be embarrassed when I heard people talking about the matching funds their companies contributed and the tremendous returns they were getting on their retirement plans. Eric, I was envious of you that you have a business of your own to provide for you future. All I have is the IRA I set up three years ago."

"How is that working out for you?" Kevin asked.

"Well, I probably shouldn't complain. After listening to Matt and Eric I feel very lucky. At least I have all the money I put in it. When I set it up I was so scared of the stock market, I had my bank set up the IRA, and basically I get their Certificate of Deposit rate. That is around 2% now. But, I have friends who opened accounts at different banks and they are getting even less."

Matt seemed to hesitate for a minute, but then he said, "Kevin, if I remember correctly, you had some real financial problems a few years ago, but now you appear to be doing great. Would you like to share your money secrets with us?"

"It actually is a secret. But since this is the last hole let's putt out, then I will share the story with ya'll; if you pay for the drinks. Matt, this was the first time I knew that Titleist even made a water seeking ball."

Matt gave his friend a look that clearly said, "That ain't even funny."

Kevin is 61 years old, and considerably older than his companions. Everyone wondered about him. It was obvious that he had been in some financial difficulties a few years back. He and his wife, Dagney had moved from a very nice, large home into a modest house half the size. They began driving a fifteen-year old car that they both referred to as their Honda POS. When asked what the POS meant they just said, "It is a Piece Of Scrap, though I have heard it described differently."

(This is the actual Honda POS. What would you have called it?)

They never talked about their circumstances. Dagney went to work for an international corporation as an Executive Assistant and Kevin was selling a contract delivery service on straight commission. Though they never changed their positive attitude, it was obvious that their circumstances had undergone some major changes.

That made it all the more noticeable when their lifestyle made another change. The Honda POS disappeared and Dagney started driving a Cadillac to work.

(Quite a step up, wouldn't you say?)

Dagney's boss saw her in the parking lot and, half-jokingly said, "Wow. Your investments must be doing great."

"As a matter of fact they are doing very well, but I am sure yours are too."

"Are you kidding? Everything I touch turns to--well you know what it turns to. Are you seriously making money from investments? You must be taking some huge risks."

"Not at all, a lot of our investments have government guaranteed interest rates of 24% and some even 50%. The others don't have a guaranteed rate but they carry very small risks and huge returns."

"Dagney, you have to be confused. There aren't any investments with guaranteed interest rates, except for things like bonds, certificates of deposit and annuities, but they are a lot closer to 2% than 24%."

"Actually, we do a lot better than 24% on most of our investments. Even my IRA earned over 68% last year, tax free."

"Look, I am the Vice President of Finance. I am a CPA. I deal in millions of dollars every day, as you well know. If there was anything out there like you just described, I would certainly know about it.

"Well, evidently not. But don't beat yourself up. Very few people know about these investment vehicles. I don't have time to go into everything, but the government guaranteed interest rates comes from Tax Lien Certificates. The rates vary from 8% to 24% depending on where you buy them, check it out."

A short while later Dagney's boss came out of his office and said, "I just called one of my college buddies who is also a CPA and asked him if he knew anything about these Tax Lien Certificates. Do you know what he told me?"

"That he hadn't heard of them either?"

"No! He said he had been investing in them for years and just assumed that I knew all about them. Since I seem to be out of the loop, what else are you and Kevin investing in that I should know about? I am almost afraid to ask if you were serious when you said that your IRA earned 68% last year."

"I was totally serious about the 68%. You aren't out of the loop, you just aren't acquainted with **The Secret Synergy Group System.** As I told you, few people know about these investments and even fewer know about The New Synergy Group. I'll be happy to talk to you about this sometime, but you probably won't do anything about it."

"My friend didn't say anything about being a member of some secret system."

"Then he obviously isn't a member. If he was, he would be making even more than he is making now, regardless of what he is making."

"Why did you say I probably won't do anything with this information?"

"To make these kinds of investments takes a minimal amount of effort. You have to do a little research. This is outside the comfort zone of most people, so they just do nothing. They feel more comfortable turning their money over to someone like a mutual fund manager than taking charge of their own money."

"I promise I am not like that. Let me take you to lunch and you can start telling me about how this works. I am curious about *this Secret Synergy Group System.* Is this some kind of cult thing?"

"Oh absolutely. We meet high in the mountains on the first night of a full moon. We dance around the trees naked until we receive inspiration from the forest fairies."

"Okay, stop. I get it, but I am still dying of curiosity."

So now Kevin finds himself in a situation similar to Dagney's. He is also willing to share the story with his friends, but he holds more hope that they will take advantage of the knowledge because he has a new resource.

So our story begins……

Chapter 1

AT THE 19TH HOLE

"The world is moving so fast these days that the man who says it can't be done is generally interrupted by someone doing it."

--- Elbert Hubbard
1856 – 1915

"Just mineral water," Kevin told the waitress.

"You only order the good stuff," Eric laughed.

"If you pay attention to what I am going to share with you, and then act on it, this will be the most life changing drink you will ever pay for. The key is to **act on it.** The greatest ideas in the world don't mean a thing unless you do something with them. Lots of people have great ideas but never do anything with them. If you want to enjoy the profits I am going to tell you about, it is going to take some effort on your part. I don't mean you are going to have to spend hours every day to make this happen; but this whole idea is to take charge of your own life. Taking charge of your money is only part of that responsibility. This is a new mindset for most people."

"This isn't going to be one of those 'Positive Thinking Will Make Everything Okay' stories is it?" Eric wanted to know.

Eric owns a small printing company that has had steady growth over the last several years. He is forty-four years old, married and has three kids. His ambition is to make sure that all three of his children are able to attend a good college without any money worries. The downturn in the economy has affected him just as it has most businesses, both large and small.

To keep his company growing, he has put almost all of the cash flow back into the business. He draws a modest salary and hasn't been able to start a college savings plan. This bothers him a lot more than he lets anyone know.

"What do you have against positive thinking?" Kevin asked.

"Absolutely nothing. I am a great believer in positive thinking. It's just that I have learned that it takes a lot more than just a great attitude to become successful."

Kevin smiled, "You are absolutely right. I can't tell you how many people I have known over the years that owned a copy of every book on positive thinking and self-improvement that was ever written. But all they ever did was read the books. You sure hit the nail on the head when you said it takes a lot more than just thinking. Remember, I said that the key to what I am going to share with you is to **act on it!**"

"But you know, no matter how positive your attitude is and how much you want to be a financial success, if you don't have the right tools it is impossible to ever get ahead. For example, which one of you guys expects to become wealthy from your job?"

All three shook their head. "Why not? All of you make pretty good money. Eric, you even own your own business. Don't you think that will make you wealthy?"

Eric was very thoughtful, "You know this is something that really concerns me. I am going to need a ton of money in a few years to educate my kids. The only way I can get that amount of money out of my business at once is to sell it. Then, I have to take whatever is left over after educating the kids and start another business. After being self-employed for all these years, I am not going to be able to get a job making the kind of money I need. So I am looking at building a brand new business again, or trying to find a job at an age when it is not realistic to think I will make as much money as I make now.

"I need to start investing in something other than my business, but everything I look at is either very risky or returns next to nothing. I really don't know what at to do. Sometimes I think the best thing is to just take the money to Vegas. It is risky, but you can get free drinks," he joked.

Aaron said, "Kevin, I think what we need to know is what you have been doing. We have never talked about it, but we knew you and Dagney went through some rough financial times but you seem to have turned your situation around in just a few years."

"You are right. We had it pretty rough for a while. But I have to admit that we had a real advantage. I was lucky enough to have worked for a man that taught me a strategy from *The Secret Synergy Group* that very few people know anything about. You know if you have the knowledge of how to make money you can achieve any goal, or overcome any setback, if you have the right attitude to go with the knowledge.

"You can't build a house or work on a car without the right tools. The tool you need to make money is knowledge. Let's see if I can illustrate what I am talking about.

"I want all of you to think about this for a minute. Where did you learn to make money? Did your parents teach you? Did you learn in high school or did they teach you in college?"

Everyone was quiet for a while. Finally Aaron spoke up, "I don't know about the rest of you, but no one ever taught me anything about making money."

Eric said, "I took some business courses in college, but they didn't teach me anything about investing. Come to think of it, they didn't teach me much about the real world of business, either."

Kevin said, "That is very typical. In school, they teach you the skills to get a job and work for someone else. They don't teach you how to be in business for yourself or how to put your money to work. But it is vital that you learn these skills somewhere. I'm going to give you some advice in a few minutes. Whether you follow my advice or not it is really important that you get the knowledge. Whether you are in business for yourself, as Eric is, or you work for a large company like Matt, you just have to learn how to make your money work."

"See, that's the problem," Matt interrupted. "No matter how much knowledge I might learn, I just don't have any extra money to invest."

"You just may have a lot more money than you think, and I will prove it to you in a few minutes," Kevin continued.

Matt took a bit of a sarcastic tone, "I just have to see this trick, given my expenses."

Kevin smiled, "Just bear with me. The first thing we have to learn is just what happens to our money."

As he spoke Kevin drew a large circle on a napkin. "Let this circle represent the lifetime earnings of the average person. I don't know how much money you guys make and it is none of my business. But the average person in America, according to recent figures, earns an average of $35,000 per year during their working years from age 25 to age 65. They often earn less when they are getting started and considerably more in later years, but the average is correct. I am pretty sure you guys all make more than this, but the percentages I am going to show you will still apply.

"Our typical American that earns $35,000 per year for forty years earns $1,400,000 in their working years. That's a fortune in anybody's book. But, let's see where it goes.

Kevin marked off a pie slice equal to a little more than one third of the circle and went on, "Taxes are going to consume around 37%, or $518,000 according to national statistics.

Kevin marked off a larger piece of the pie and wrote 44% in the slice, "Interest over a lifetime will consume 44% of the total income. This includes interest on homes, cars, various loans, credit cards....the list goes on and on, but I think you get the picture.

"Most people are shocked when they see this and many just disagree. Bear in mind these are average figures, but when you get home just look at your mortgage loan and car loan statements and see how much interest you are paying. Most people are shocked.

"So now 81% of the total income is gone, and we haven't bought a loaf of bread."

Aaron looked at the napkin in disbelief. "I'm just 29 years old. Do you mean this is what I have to look forward to?"

"Only if you choose," Kevin answered.

"You mean I have a choice?"

"Oh, you have lots of choices. Remember I said it is important to learn about money and how to make it work for you? Is everyone starting to get the picture?"

"This sure isn't very encouraging," Matt murmured.

"Cheer up. Remember, I said it doesn't have to be this way," Kevin laughed.

"But let's go on. So far our average person, who doesn't learn what you guys are going to learn, has paid $518,000 in taxes and spent $615,000 in interest. Bear in mind, these amounts will change for people who make more or less than the average, but the percentages are the same.

"Now hang on. The news gets worse for many people. They only have 19% of disposable income to maintain the family and educate the kids. This is why credit card debt and bankruptcies are both increasing at an alarming rate.

"I have rounded off the percentages, but this leaves $267,000 for our average person. If they work the typical forty-hour week, they earn an average of $3.21 per hour. Their actual spendable income is about half the minimum wage.

"Now you see why people don't get ahead just on their salary. They really have to take some of their money and put it to work. Then they have to make sure that money works just as hard as they worked to earn it."

"I don't see how that $3.21 is going to do much heavy lifting," Eric said. "I think most families have two incomes, but I can see that doubling their income is still not going to leave much to put to work. So what are they, I mean we, going to do?"

"The first thing you have to do is get some specialized knowledge about making money," Kevin answered. "As I told you earlier, I am going to suggest a source, but whether you take my advice or not, you really have to gain some knowledge of how money works from someone.

"Most people don't get ahead because they just won't invest in themselves. They will buy cars, boats, golf clubs, huge TV sets and all sorts of toys, but they won't spend a nickel on a book, or a seminar or courses at a Community

College that just addresses ways to make money. I have heard it said that poor people have large TVs and rich people have large libraries."

"Yeah, but aren't most of those books and seminars just scams," Aaron asked.

"Quite frankly, a lot of them are," Kevin answered. "But just because there are some bad apples, it doesn't mean they are all bad. There is a lot of good information out there; you just need to learn how to tell the difference.

"I am going to recommend a financial planner. Not just any financial planner. The typical financial planner isn't going to know anything about the things I am going to share with you now. There is only one financial planner in our area that really understands these programs and techniques. Her name is Lauren Taggert.

"If you think the only ways to invest are stocks, bonds, mutual funds, real estate and bank accounts Lauren isn't the planner for you. But if you are open to some proven, but little known programs she will open your eyes like a wide-angle lens. She is not going to recommend a specific investment. The typical broker or planner will try to sell you on investing in a specific company or mutual fund.

"But Lauren subscribes to the notion that if you give a man a fish, you feed him for a day, but if you teach him how to fish you feed him for a lifetime. She will teach you programs and techniques. She will teach you how to research specific opportunities, but she won't make that decision for you. You need to be willing to do some work on your own.

"This sounds like it is going to involve a lot of learning and require a lot of time," Eric frowned.

Kevin shook his head, "No more than what you should take on any investment. The average investor invests in things they couldn't answer two questions about. They don't know the difference between an option and a warrant, or the difference between a put and a call. Yet they buy stocks and mutual funds all the time. Then they scream like a stepped on cat when they get stuck with a bunch of Enron stock or scammed by a Bernie Madoff.

"You are kind of making this sound like some off the wall investments, and what about this *'Secret Synergy Group System?'*" It was obvious that Aaron wasn't comfortable.

"It is about much more than one thing, but believe me Lauren will give you all the information you need to check out any and all of these programs," Kevin answered, then he laughed, "As for the *'Secret Synergy Group System'* she will explain that too. But don't get worked up over it. You aren't going to be charged any dues nor attend any strange meetings. Certainly not anything as strange as the *'Skull and Bones'* that some of our presidents have belonged to.

"Let me give you an example. Are you aware that you can buy government receivables that carry interest rates of anywhere between 8% and 24%? Did you know that you can choose the interest rate you want? Did you know these interest rates are guaranteed by the government and the government can't let them go down? What if you could make these investments without ever getting off your couch? Would that be a good deal?"

"Whoa, this is starting to sound like one of that pie in the sky deals to me," Eric said. "I'm sure no investment expert, but I have never heard of anything like this. Kevin I have a lot of respect for you, but please don't suggest some far out deal, I am far too conservative for anything like that. But because of my regard for you I do want to know what you are talking about."

"Good! I am glad you are skeptical, because I was too when I first heard of this program. After all we live in a land of instant coffee, instant tea and instant disbelief. But sometimes things are just as they are presented.

"What I am going to share with you now is information that you will not get from your banker, broker, CPA or any other investment advisor."

"If the experts don't know about these investments, or aren't comfortable in recommending them, how can I have confidence in them?" Matt was obviously troubled.

"Okay, while everyone is in this great skeptical mood, let me just make you a lot more skeptical," Kevin smiled. It was obvious that this was just the reaction he expected from his friends and he was taking great delight in toying with them.

"If you were skeptical before, I may as well warp your mind for good. Aaron, you said your IRA is earning around 3%, right?"

"That's right."

"Matt you said you had what's left of your 401k in a money market account at around 2%, is that right?"

"Yeah, something like that."

"Well you are actually very fortunate. Many of these accounts are paying less than 1%. I don't mean to be critical, but your money would do about as well in a safe deposit box. At least you would know you aren't going to lose it.

"I don't like to share personal information, and I hope this doesn't go past you guys, but Dagney and I have IRAs that earned over 60% last year."

"No Way!" everyone said, almost in unison. They had all been leaning forward listening to Kevin, but when he said his IRA earned over 60% they all leaned back in disbelief at the same time.

"Actually some of our investments do even better. But before we go on, let me just assure you that anyone can do what we are doing. As I mentioned before it takes some knowledge and some work. Dagney and I do this full time now, but we didn't make it a full time job until the income from our investments exceeded the income from our jobs by more than 50%. We got to that point working at it part time."

"How much time did you spend when this was a part time business?" Aaron wanted to know.

"In the beginning it was about an hour a day because we had very little money or time to invest. The time was spent doing research. That is not as difficult as it might sound. All our research is done on line. Now we only spend as much time as necessary. I really enjoy poking around in a

Page | 33

lot of options so I will sometimes work eight or ten hours one day and then maybe nothing for a few days. Our objective is to keep all our money working all the time. It is like a really great game.

"Now back to the business of warping your mind. If you believe one word of what I am about to tell you before you check it out, you are nuts. I certainly wouldn't believe such a wild story, if I didn't already know it is routine for members of *'The Secret Synergy Group System.'* "
"Not with this secret system business again," Matt complained.

"Oh, but it is necessary because only members get this special treatment. This is how Dagny and I get such huge earnings on our IRA and other accounts.

"For example what if you agreed to accept just ¼ of 1% (.25%) and after you invested your money the government came back to you and said, 'Here is the money you invested at .25%, but we insist that you accept a 60% annualized return. Here is your check?'

"What if you dealt with another government agency and you said you would be happy with 18% but after six months the government comes back and insists you accept 36%? Then six months later they come back and say you have to accept 54%. Another six months goes by and they are knocking on the door again to force you to accept 72%. This continues until they return with their final demand that you accept 108%.

"Or what if you think a 50% annualized yield is OK but you have to take a 300% yield because it is the law?"

Aaron got everyone's attention because he was chuckling so. "Kevin you certainly lived up to your promise. I don't believe a single word you say. Where is the punch line?"

"Good for you Aaron, that is just where you should be, so let's start making some sense of all this.

"Remember, I said there was more than one program? Let me start by just giving you an overview of these government receivables. These are the easiest and require the least amount of time.
"Has anyone ever heard of a Tax Lien Certificate? You are all shaking your heads and that puts you among the vast majority of Americans. As I said I am just going to acquaint you with what they are. Then if you have some interest and will convince me that you will follow through, I will introduce you to Lauren.

"Here is what a Tax Lien Certificate does, and then I will tell you what it is.

"If you want to have some fun, try this. Go to a stockbroker, real estate broker, or anyone that sells investments. Or go to your banker for some advice.

"Believe me they will break a leg to dust off a chair for you. Who knows: they might even offer you coffee.

"Now explain that your investment has to meet certain standards. If you can get a word in edgeways when they start assuring you that their particular investments are of the highest standards; you continue.

"You explain that you want to control an investment portfolio of over $10,000,000. Now watch the drool drip off their chins.

"But," you say, "I only want to invest $130,000 today." As they are rubbing their hands together and the vision of huge commissions dancing in their head, you continue," "But I absolutely insist that this $130,000 gives me control over $10,000,000 in assets.

"As they sputter to explain that this just isn't possible you say, "Wait, I'm not finished. I also want to earn at least 24% on some of my investment, I want that rate guaranteed by the government to not go down and, oh, by the way, I will want some of my investment capital to earn a guaranteed rate of 50%

"Now it is no longer funny to them. They are ready to call security to get the guys in the white coats, you continue. "Just one other thing, in the event the investment doesn't quite work out the way we want, I expect to receive the $10,000,000 in assets to do with as I wish even though I will never invest more than $130,000."

"While they are waiting for the ambulance to carry you away, they want to know where you ever got such a crazy idea. You say, 'I do it all the time, don't you? I just invest in Tax Lien Certificates.'

Now don't get excited you could invest $13,000 and control $1,000,000 or $1,300 and control $130,000. You could even invest less than $50.

"That is what a Tax Lien Certificate does. Now let me explain what a Tax Lien Certificate is.   Tax Lien certificates are created by State Legislatures and are primarily issued by county governments. There are some city governments and even some school districts that also issue and sell Tax Lien Certificates. But the far greater percentage of them are issued and sold by counties, so from her on we will only speak of counties just for simplicity.

Kevin was in his element at this point. He is so enthusiastic about Tax Lien Certificates that he just loves to tell others about them. Everyone listened with total attention as he explained what Tax Lien Certificates are and the wonderful opportunities they carry.

He began by explaining that most counties receive more than half their income from property taxes. The county establishes a budget and taxes real property to fund the majority of their budget. Each taxpayer receives a notice of the taxes due. Sometimes a property owner is either unable or unwilling to pay the taxes on time. Delinquent taxes become a lien on the real estate.

When these taxes aren't paid on time, this creates a shortfall in the county budget. Since the counties need the money right away, the legislatures in some thirty-three states created a way for the counties to receive the money without waiting for the taxpayer to eventually pay.

The county has two very special rights, as far as the taxpayer is concerned. The owner of the real estate has to either pay the taxes, or the county can take the property. This is true in all states. But these Tax Lien Certificate states established an interim step. The states created a debt instrument, a government receivable that the counties could sell to a private investor for the amount of the taxes. For example, if the taxes due are $1,000 a Tax Lien Certificate for $1,000 is created for sale to investor.

To make this instrument saleable to investors the state laws in these states pass all the rights granted to the counties along to this certificate.

Remember that these rights are to receive the taxes or take the property. So the owner of a Tax Lien Certificate has the same rights as the county. They either get back all they invested, plus a high rate of interest, or they get the property.

The states established an interest rate that must be paid along with the taxes. Different states established different rates. They vary from 8% in Oklahoma to 24% in Iowa. The counties hold an auction, usually once each year and sell these certificates to investors.

The purchaser of one of these certificates pays the county $1,000, in our examples, and now has the right to receive the $1,000 plus the interest rate set by the state, or they have the right to take the property and do whatever they wish with it.

The county has the money for their budget and the investor is either going to receive all his money back along with a high rate of interest, or he will take the property.

"Are you saying you invest in these receivables and actually take people's homes away from them?" Eric was clearly troubled by this prospect.

"It doesn't work quite like that," Kevin laughed.

Kevin went on to explain that when the states established the interest rate on these taxes due, they also established a redemption period. This is a period of time, a grace period if you will, that the taxpayer has to pay all the taxes due, along with all the interest and have the lien released. Just as the interest rate varies, this redemption period also varies from state to state.

"Rarely does anyone lose their home or the family farm this way," Kevin explained. "Who is going to lose a $100,000 house for a $1,000 tax bill? But, if this happens it is not the fault of the investor. That taxpayer would have lost the real estate to the county anyway. The investor is in no way taking advantage of anyone.

"I'll bet I know what your next question is: 'If I buy one of these certificates do I have to collect the taxes?' Am I right?" Eric, Matt and Aaron all nodded their heads.

"Actually an investor never even meets the property owner. The taxes are still paid at the County Treasurer's Office. (In some states called Tax Collector) The county then forwards the amount of the taxes, and all the interest that was due and collected, to the investor.

"For example Mississippi certificates carry a 17% interest rate and there is a two year redemption period. So anytime, during the two-year period, the taxpayer can bring the taxes and interest current and the lien is released.

"Remember, these interest rates cannot go down. They are set by law."

Matt said, "Wow, I really like these rates of interest, but this sounds terribly complicated."

Page | 39

"Actually, it isn't complicated at all, but you do have to learn of some potential pitfalls. You also have to learn how to bid, because they are sold in different forms of public auctions. You need to know how to protect your interest after you invest. If you decide to pursue this, Lauren will give you all the details and she will show you how to buy in states without ever going there. You never have to get off your couch."

"Wait, wait, wait!" It was Eric who asked, "I am getting confused on a couple of issues. First you talk about buying at auctions. Then you tell us we don't even have to get off our duff. Which is it?"

"Both. Lots of counties hold their auctions online but some still have live auctions where you must be present to bid. Members of *The Secret Synergy Group System* sometimes even buy by mail.

"There you go with that secret business again. I am not sure if I am anxious to find out about this or if I should be scared." Eric was laughing, but it was a nervous laugh.

"I told you I am confused on a couple of issues. You answered the first one but my second source of confusion is how the 17% interest rate you just mentioned turned into 60% in your IRA. This sounds like a smoke and mirror deal that may be the same story the government is trying to feed us."

"Well we do invest in Tax Lien Certificates, as I told you. If fact they are the foundation of our entire investment plans. But that is not the end of the story.

"I told you that some thirty three states have created and sell Tax Lien Certificates. The other states do it a little differently. When a taxpayer has been delinquent for some period of time, which varies, not just by state, but also from county to county, the county takes the property directly and sells it at auction.

"This creates a lot of great opportunities. These properties are routinely bought at auction from the county for 50% to 70% of their Fair Market Value. Sometimes they are bought for much less.

"Some of these states auction the property and also impose a penalty interest rate. There are many ways to buy property at huge discounts because of a problem with taxes. Dagney and I quite often buy through our Roth IRAs, or one of our other tax shelters."

Matt still looked puzzled, "I'm really lost. I have looked at a lot of ways to set up an IRA. I looked at the bank, my insurance company and several mutual funds. None of them ever mentioned anything like this."

"That's because none of these companies offer a truly Self-Directed IRA. Some of them call their accounts self-directed, but when you check in to it you will find that you can only direct your money into the family of mutual funds that they sell. For example you can direct your funds into a Fidelity Small Cap Fund, or you can direct that money into an overseas fund, but still with Fidelity.

"Dagney and I have a completely Self-Directed IRA. We can invest our funds anywhere we want as long as the IRS doesn't prohibit our choice. We buy real estate and invest in Tax Lien Certificates through our IRA. We even use our

Page | 41

IRA as a bank and make loans at substantial interest rates. I don't have time to go into all the particulars and that is Lauren's job anyway. But an IRA is so much more than people know. It is amazing what you can do when you know how."

"Yeah, when we are members of *The Secret Synergy Group System,* right?" Aaron was pretty sure he knew the answer.

Aaron looked at the others and asked, "Are you guys following all this? I am getting excited about the possibilities, but I'm not totally sure what I am excited about. So Kevin, when do we meet this Lauren? She sounds like someone that I certainly want to know."

"I'll call today and set up a meeting. But let me tell you; you need to be totally serious and committed if you decide to go all the way. My suggestion is that Lauren meets with all three of you and your wives together to save time. She will completely explain her philosophy, how the programs work and her fees. If you are still interested at that point, she can set up individual private meetings. How does that sound?" Everyone nodded their agreement.

"Great why don't you all talk with your wives then call me and let me know the time and I will coordinate it with Lauren."

Matt was rubbing his hands together, "I can't wait. From what you have told us Kevin, this is going to be mind boggling.

"And from the pleased look on Kevin's face I get the feeling that there may be a lot more than what he has told us so far. Is that right Kevin?"

"Oh, a lot more."

"Aaron frowned, "I just hope I have the money to take advantage of some of these programs."

Kevin said, "Put your mind at ease. What if I told you that soda pop from the fridge and a brown bag lunch could make you rich? Then what if I told you that you could buy $10,000 to $50,000 chunks of real estate for $25 to $100?

"Would you be surprised if I told you that you could start investing in Tax Lien Certificates with probably less money that you have in your pocket right now?

"While you are all picking your jaws up off the floor, I am going to take my leave. Call me after you guys agree on a time."

"Just one more quick question. Why don't other investment advisors know about this? In fact if these are sponsored by the government why doesn't everyone know about them, and how long has this been going on?" Eric wanted to know.

Kevin had expected this question, "Eric, this is the best kept, publicly advertised, secret in the world. In fact newspapers publish lists of the liens for sale usually thirty days before the sale but people don't know what they are so they just head for the sports section. The government is under no obligation to educate the public about these.

"As to why investment advisors and brokers don't sell them, it is very simple. They can't get a commission. You buy them from the government, the government collects the money and the government pays you. Couldn't be simpler.

"How long they have been around? I am not sure. I did find out that Thomas Jefferson and his friends were buying them prior to 1776 so I assume the idea was brought over from Europe. It is all there in Jefferson's biography.

"Now, I really do have to go, Dagney will think I have a girl friend."

Chapter 2

THE VIEW FROM 30,000 FEET

"It is a lesson which all history teaches wise men, to put trust in ideas, and not in circumstances."

Ralph Waldo Emerson

"Wait. Let me get this straight. You want me to go with you, to meet with some lady you heard about on the golf course that is going to make us rich? How much Amway product do I have to sell?"

"First of all, it wasn't just something I overheard on the golf course. Kevin Daniels told me, Aaron and Matt about her today. And I didn't say she was going to make us rich. Apparently Kevin and Dagney have a long history with her and her advice. It appears they have done OK."

"Only if you think a gorgeous home on a forty acre estate with an indoor pool and Dagney's Rolls Royce is called 'OK.'"

"You forgot the twin engine plane."

"Yes I did forget. So if you throw in the plane, I will agree they are doing 'OK!'" Allison laughed.

Eric Taylor had just mentioned to his wife Allison that they were supposed to coordinate with Matt and Malone along with Aaron and his wife Patricia, or Trish as they all called her, for a meeting with the mystery planner, Lauren.

Similar conversations were taking place with Aaron and Trish and with Matt and Malone.

"Are you saying that Kevin told you guys this lady helped him and Dagney go from a thirty year old house and a fifteen year old Honda to that gorgeous place where they live now?"

"He didn't say it in those words, but he indicated that she played an important role in their fortune."

"You devil, you know how curious I am about everything so I've got to meet this financial genius. When do we meet?"

Eric said, "He would like to introduce all of us to her at the same time at his house. He said she would give us an overview and then if we decide we want to pursue this she will meet with each couple privately at a later date. We won't be making a commitment by just meeting her.

"Besides, he said we could all go swimming after the meeting while he prepares a barbecue dinner for us."

Allison was already heading for the phone. "Great I'm calling Malone and Trish right now and get this planned."

It was Saturday afternoon two weeks after the golf outing. The doorbell had just rung, or rather made the sound of an oriental gong and Kevin excused himself from the others to answer the door.

"Aaron, Trish! You two come on in. The others are here. I want you to meet Lauren and her husband Henry."

Trish was slightly embarrassed, "Are we late? We were just exploring the area. All the homes here are so beautiful."

Kevin gave her a hug and said, "Of course you aren't late and you are right, there are some nice homes in the area."

Aaron chuckled, "Are all your neighbors members of this *Secret Synergy Group System?*"

"As a matter of fact a couple of them are." Kevin answered. "We are here to talk about you, so come on in and let's get acquainted."

While Kevin introduced the last couple to the guest of honor, Dagney brought refreshments for everyone and they were all seated in front of a massive fireplace.

Lauren stood with her back to the fireplace facing everyone. Behind her was a large Bev Doolittle painting called *"The Forest Has Eyes."* Allison made a mental note to ask Dagney about the painting after the meeting.

Kevin addressed the group, "Before we get started I want to share something with you. This is from a letter that the Wall Street Journal has mailed to solicit new subscriptions for years. It just seems appropriate for our meeting. Here is what it says:

'On a beautiful late spring afternoon, twenty-five years ago, two young men graduated from the same college. They were very much alike, these two young men.

'Both had been better than average students, both were personable and both – as young college graduates are – were filled with ambitious dreams for the future.

'Recently, these men returned to their college for their 25ᵗʰ reunion.

'They were still very much alike.

'Both were happily married. Both had three children. And both, it turned out, had gone to work for the same Midwestern manufacturing company after graduation, and were still there.

'But there was a difference. One of the men was a manager of a small department of that company. The other was its president.

What Made The Difference

'Have you ever wondered, as I have, what makes this kind of difference in people's lives? It isn't always a native

intelligence or talent or dedication. It isn't that one person wants success and the other doesn't.

'The difference –

Kevin paused and said, "Everyone pay particular attention to this next statement from the Journal story." He continued reading very slowly.

---lies in what each person knows and how he or she makes use of that knowledge.'

"Friends I believe this is the major difference between success and failure. Lauren is going to open your eyes to some knowledge that you never knew existed until our golf game a couple of weeks ago.

"Lauren can give you the knowledge, but it is totally up to you what you do with it.

"So now that I have had my little three minutes of attention, Lauren will give you an overview of what is in store for any, or all of you, who take advantage of the knowledge."

Lauren began, "Before I start sharing with you what we do and how we work I want to ask a favor of all of you. Each of you have a pad and one of Kevin's special pens with his KD brand on it. I want you to make very good use of the pads and pens tonight.

"I have heard lots of speakers begin with the statement, 'Just set your disbelief aside until I have finished.' Well I want you to do just the opposite. Please do not believe one word you hear here tonight. Not until I have proven it to you. I am going to share some things with you that you would have to take leave of your senses to believe.

"I am going to give you reference information where you can look up everything I tell you so that you are completely comfortable that everything is exactly the way I tell you. If you can't get comfortable with any part of it you should never do business with me, or with anyone else that raises a speck of doubt, for that matter.

"I will not try to convince you that the things I will share are possible. I am going to tell you positively that they are not only possible; they are totally routine to the people who understand them. Fair enough?" After everyone had nodded their agreement she continued, "I want you to look up the proof yourselves"

Lauren's air of confidence and appearance kept everyone's attention completely focused. She was almost five foot ten, with very dark brown hair and striking green eyes. She was wearing casual black wool slacks and a white long sleeved tuxedo blouse with a large turned up collar and short heeled black alligator shoes.

An altogether striking appearance, but her voice and her delivery were her most noticeable features. She had a voice only slightly deeper than most women, but when she spoke it projected an air of authority that commanded attention.

"The information I am going to share with you this afternoon only has to do with the tools you can use, if you choose, to attain any level of wealth you want. As Kevin stressed, a tool means nothing. It is only what you do with it.

"Kevin has told me enough about all of you for me to know that you are the type of people who can be successful – the only kind I will work with.

"Just keep your eye on what is important and not the amount of money you can readily accumulate. Think about how your future can be. It is strictly up to you.

"Eric, I would like you and Allison to picture yourselves at your children's graduation from university. Kevin has told me enough for me to know how important that is for you.

"I understand that Kevin has given you the basics of Tax Lien Certificates but let me illustrate what happens with some real life examples."

Kevin had set up a large screen TV on a stand just to the left of where Lauren was speaking. She clicked a remote control and a nice middle class, two story house with a three car garage appeared on the screen.

Lauren continued, "Here is an example. The house on the screen is in Denver. The owner, for whatever reason, did not pay the real estate taxes of $1,636.95. The house is easily worth $200,000 even in this depressed market.

"Since the taxes weren't paid a lien was created on the property. The county owns the lien. The lien gives the county two rights: to collect these taxes, or they can take the property. This is true in every state. However different states handle the enforcement of these rights differently.

"As Kevin told you, about half the states have enacted laws to allow the County Government to collect the amount of taxes due by selling their rights to the Tax Lien to an investor. This is done by creating an instrument that gives an investor who buys the lien the same rights the county has. This is called a Tax Lien Certificate.

"A Tax Lien Certificate in the amount of **$1,636.95** that carried a 14% interest rate was sold on this exact house. The investor will get the $1,636.95 plus 14% interest or he could own the house. Now it is more involved than what we have time to explain this afternoon, but it is very simple. I will explain it in complete detail to any of you who wish to pursue this past our meeting this afternoon.

Lauren clicked again. This time a very modest, but well-kept house appeared. "Tax Lien Certificates are sold in all denominations. For example here is a small house in a nice, working-class, neighborhood. The Tax Lien Certificate was only **$534.45**. The house is worth around $100,000.

"That's my finger in front of the lens; it isn't included."

P

Malone whispered to Matt, "That looks just like the house Kevin and Dagney lived in before they moved here."

Matt shushed her, but nodded in agreement.

They both avoided looking at Kevin and Dagney at this point so they didn't see Kevin squeeze Dagney's hand and give it a small shake at the sight of the house.

The next click brought up a three story condominium complex. "One of the condos in this development had a Tax Lien Certificate sold for just **$97.82**."

She clicked again, "Here is a warehouse worth over a million dollars. A Tax Lien Certificate was sold for **$137,934.17**." As she spoke she showed a picture of a warehouse with offices in the front in an industrial district.

"These are actual properties and the amounts of the Tax Liens were taken directly from public records. What all these examples have in common is that the taxes will be paid to the county, along with the interest due, then the county will send both the amount of the taxes and the interest along to the investor and the lien is cleared.

"If the taxes aren't paid the holder of the Tax Lien Certificate will own the property. Steps to ownership vary from state to state. We will cover the steps for those that continue in the program.

"In this quick example you have seen liens for less than $100 to over $100,000. Everyone can invest in Tax Lien Certificates. If you choose to pursue these opportunities you will learn things that can be done with Tax Lien Certificates that few people ever imagine.

"Remember, I told you to not believe anything I tell you. Check it out for yourself. So before we go any further please write down this web address: www.wowworks.com

"On the left side of the home page at that address is a list of states. Click on any state, but for our illustration click on Colorado. Then click on Adams County. From there go to the Treasurer's site and look at the information on Tax Lien Certificate sales. There you will get the confidence in what Kevin has shared, and what I am about to tell you is absolutely true.

"You can do this basic research for most of the counties in the country. But you will recall that not all counties sell Tax Lien Certificates and not all counties have searchable websites.

"Kevin, did you explain how they can choose their own rate of interest?"

"I mentioned that it is possible to choose, but I didn't explain how it is done."

"Some of you may have already figured out how to choose the interest rate. As you have learned interest rates vary from state to state. You just choose the state that has the interest rate that you need and buy Tax Lien Certificates in that state. You needn't live in the state and in most counties you can buy online so you never need get off your couch."

Allison spoke up, "Which state imposes the highest interest rate?"

Lauren smiled, "Allison I think I know where you are going with that question. It seems logical to just pick the state with the highest rate and just buy certificates in that state, right?"

"Works for me." Allison nodded.

"First let me give you the short answer. The highest rate imposed by a state is 24% in Iowa. There are a couple of other places where you can get 24% also. But rate is not always the determining factor."

"What other factors?" Allison looked puzzled.

"Well the period of time you have to hold the certificate before you can get the property, if that is what you are after. Also how simple or complicated is the deed process after the redemption period. The redemption period is the period, from six months to five years, depending on the state, that the property owner has to pay the taxes and interest.

"That's one factor and you will learn them all. But here is just a quick consideration for buying in Iowa, while we are on that subject.

"Because the rate is so high, there is a lot of competition among investors. Iowa has a couple of other quirks that you will want to learn about before you invest there. But it is an excellent place to own Tax Lien Certificates."

"Kevin, may I share with them your favorite state and why you and Dagney invest there?"

Kevin nodded and Lauren continued, "Kevin and Dagney like Arizona for a few reasons. First of all the interest rate is very good; 16%. The redemption period is three years and there are always lots of certificates for sale.

"But there is even a better reason. Dagney is a native of Arizona. Her father still lives there so they like to visit as often as possible. Since they have both Tax Lien Certificates and real estate there; the trips they take to Arizona are partly tax deductible as a business expense because they are looking after their investments and exploring more possibilities. I will teach you how this is possible.

"So to be as successful as possible you need a plan and then you fit the Tax Lien Certificates that will get you to your goal into that plan. If you are just buying Tax Lien Certificates hither and yon, you will make money. But if you have a logical plan you will make infinitely more money.

"So let's look at an example. Assume that your plan calls for your investments to provide you with enough money to live the lifestyle you choose twenty years from now. My philosophy calls for Tax Lien Certificates to be the foundation to your financial house because the rates are guaranteed. You will learn other strategies that can cut your time in half, or less, but Tax Lien Certificates are the only vehicle that carries such high interest rates with a guarantee.

"For simplicity sake, let's assume that you will need to have $75,000 per year in income that has a guaranteed rate. How much capital do you need, and what interest rate will accomplish this?

"We talked about Arizona so let's use that state and their 16% interest rate for our illustration. We divide the $75,000 by 16% and find we will need $468,750 to provide our income goal.

"Now I go to my Texas Instrument BA35 calculator and find that I will need to invest $4,062 per year for 20 years at 16% to accumulate $468,750. We are within IRA contribution limits. So we set up a Roth IRA and we are in a position to have $75,000 per year tax free annual income in 20 years.

"Just for fun, let's see what we would have with the same annual contributions and the same twenty years if we invested in Florida at 18%. It is just 2% more in interest rates, so you wouldn't think there would be much difference.

"Let's see. Back to the calculator and we find we would accumulate $595,602 and have positioned ourselves for $107,208 annual, tax free, income. This is a 43% increase in annual income. $32,000 per year more with only a 2% increase in rate. Amazing what a small difference in interest rates can make."

Aaron had been totally absorbed in what Lauren was saying, but he looked troubled. "This is all really great, if a person can afford to do it. Trish and I are just keeping our heads above water, so the four thousand dollars would be a real struggle. I would really like to do this, but I just don't see how. Trish would have to go to work and that would spoil the plan we have for the kids to always have one parent at home. We don't want to sacrifice their time just so we can have a better time later on. What do we do?"

Kevin spoke up, "Pardon me for interrupting Lauren but this is probably a good time for the soda pop from the fridge plan. Aaron, do you remember that I told you that a brown bag lunch and soda pop from the fridge could make you rich?"

"Yeah, but I thought you were just kidding."

Kevin smiled at Lauren and said, "This is your show, how about explaining this to everyone."

Almost in unison everyone said, "This I've gotta hear."

"Okay, maybe we can use Aaron for a real life example. Aaron do you buy your lunch each day?"

"Yes, most days.

"Even if you go to a fast food joint each day that has to cost at least $3.00 every doesn't it?"

"Oh at least that much, usually more."

"Let's just use the $3.00 as an average. That's $15 per week, or $780 per year. Aaron, I am not going to suggest that you skip lunch, but what if you brought your lunch from home? You can do that for half what the hamburger and drink costs, so you can save $390 per year.

"Do you ever stop at a convenience store and get a Big Gulp, or whatever they sell, or even go to Starbucks."

"I sometimes get a cold drink to take back to work with me after lunch."

"I'm going to be real generous here. You are going to spend an average of at least $1.25 per day. I know it is more but you said you stop 'sometimes.'

"If you bought your drinks at the grocery store and brought them with you; you could save at least $.75 per day, which is $3.75 per week or $195 per year.

"Okay let's add this up. If you add the $195 from the drinks to the $390 from lunch, you are up to $585 per year. Not all the money in the world. But what if just this small amount was invested in Illinois Tax Lien Certificates, they pay 18% and more, for 20 years in a Roth Ira?

"Are you ready for this? That's a whopping $85,777! All this for just a brown bag sandwich and canned soda pop.

"It gets better. At the end of the 20 years you can start cashing in enough Tax Lien Certificates to pay yourself 18% per year on the $85,777. That's $15,439 per year or

$1,286 per month. These are approximate figures; they may vary slightly in real life.

Then re-invest the new interest earnings to keep your capital intact. "Folks, this is what Aaron, who worried that he had no money to invest can do. If this sounds like you, just know that those Whoppers and designer coffees are costing you over $1,000 per month in future income. I really hope they are that good."

"Wow, I never dreamed something this simple could make that much difference, Eric I am packing your lunch tomorrow," Allison laughed.

"Oh, that is just a start for those that decide to participate," Lauren said. "You are going to learn to reset the temperature on your water heater and increase retirement income $220 per month.

"Learn the correct way to buy car insurance and add $84 per month to your retirement, and we haven't even mentioned your $250,000 cars."

The last statement caused quite a stir. Malone said, "No one here drives a $250,000 car. Well, except for Dagney."

"You will learn how the car you are driving now could be costing you that much. Whether you buy a $250,000 car is another matter." Lauren said.

Dagney spoke up "If you remember I drove the POS for years long before I got Tootsie Rolls. Kevin gave me a challenge a couple of years ago to make $250,000 on a single real estate deal and we would buy me a Rolls and I could name it Tootsie."

Lauren got serious again, "You never know what you can do until you gain the correct knowledge and stick to a plan that is right for you.

"We have only talked about one weapon you need in your arsenal. You will learn many more. For instance, you will learn to buy properties from the state at 50% discounts, and sometimes even 90%.

"You will learn how a two paragraph letter will have people calling you to offer their property for $100 or less when you show them that selling you the property for so little will add at least $1,500 spendable dollars to their income for years.

"I don't think I am talking out of school, but Kevin told me how one of these letters brought him a phone call from a gentleman in Indiana who wanted to give him a three unit apartment house. Is that right Kevin?"

"Totally correct, Kevin agreed. "But I didn't accept the deal. You will learn how to tell the good deals from the bad ones, regardless of price, later on."

Lauren continues, "These strategies are just a start. You will learn to get unlimited funding for your deals without ever applying for a loan."

"So is that what this *Secret Synergy Group System* is all about?" Matt asked.

Lauren said, "Let's just hold information about the System until you have a plan. Today we were talking primarily about Tax Lien Certificates and I gave you a website where you can look up information from a typical county for yourself. If we get together later, I will give similar information for everything I tell you."

"This is the beginning of the way I construct financial plans. You will learn things that will make you even more money and many times quicker. They carry almost zero risk. Actually as close to zero as you can get, but they do not carry a government guaranteed interest rate.

"But if you have a solid bedrock of Tax Lien Certificates underneath them, even if you should fail to make money in another investment you still have your safety net. There is just no substitute for this strategy that I have ever heard about.

"I wish there was time to get into some of these other strategies but to be fair to them it takes more time than we have this afternoon.

"We will immediately start a plan to increase your present monthly income. We will give you a plan to get you debt free in three years and have your house paid off in seven years.

"But always bear in mind that you are just learning the tools and how to use them. If you choose, I will mentor you and coach you, but all the decisions are up to you. You just have to be totally committed and follow through. How you do anything, is how you do everything, so you need to be in until you reach your goals and beyond.

"I am not going to ask for a show of hands because this is an individual decision, but if two of you, or all three, decide to take the next step I have a suggestion. This is just a suggestion and if you are not comfortable with it we can do it another way.

'The initial information you will be receiving will be the same for each of you. Eric you and Allison will get the same information on Tax Lien Certificates, Tax Deeds etc. as Matt and Malone or Aaron and Trish.

'So if you would like, we can have our first meeting all together. I have found that works very well when everyone is as compatible as you all seem to be. One of you will ask a question that the others might not think of. Of course discussion of individual situations and goals are strictly between each of you and me.

'Talk it over, then one of you can call me when you decide and we will set up the meeting. If that doesn't work, each of you can call me for individual sessions."

At this point Kevin stood up, "Okay, I know Lauren has given you a lot to think about and created about a million questions in your minds but let's give her a rest. I invited you here primarily to hear Lauren. But we want to have some fun at the same time. The pool is open and I will be taking steak orders.

"If you forgot your swim suit, Dagney will show you the closet in the pool room where there are lots of suits to choose from. You will definitely find one in your size.

"So let's give Lauren a big hand for what she did here this afternoon. Take time to get acquainted with her and Hank. You will come to treasure them as friends the same as Dagney and I have. Enjoy.

Chapter 3

HERE IS WHERE IT STARTS

"Gentlemen, we are going back to the basics; this is a football." ---Vince Lombardi addressing the Green Bay Packers after they had a bad game

After lots of fun in the pool and a great meal all three couples said thanks to Dagney and Kevin and left only moments apart.

Within minutes of leaving, Allison, Malone and Trish were on a cell phone conference call.

All three ladies were very excited and readily agreed that it would be great for all three couples to meet with Lauren at the same time.

"Did I understand Lauren correctly? Did she say she would show us how to be debt free in three years and have our mortgage loan paid off in seven years?" Malone asked the other two ladies.

"That's what she said. She also said she could show us how to get an immediate increase in take home pay without asking for a raise or working overtime. That really got my attention and Matt's too." Malone said.

Allison interjected, "You know I really hope we aren't getting our hopes up for nothing. Usually when something sounds too good to be true, it is. In fact I don't think I would even be interested if it weren't for Kevin and Dagney."

Even though everyone was impressed with Lauren, it was the respect for Kevin and Dagney that carried the day. A time was set the following week to begin the journey.

Both Kevin and Lauren had promised everyone that they would learn absolutely everything they will need in order to have complete confidence in themselves and the strategies.

Lauren had learned through experience that anyone investing in the products she was teaching, positively had to understand the basics, and the basic product in her teachings is Tax Lien Certificates.

Her protégés, as she referred to them did not need to be experts. She told them, "I am not going to bore you with more information than you need. You want to make money, not become an expert on county government. But you do need to learn this, so just grit your teeth and let's go."

It was actually painless and each of the couples had no problem paying attention to what Lauren was teaching.

So she began.

"Counties assess taxes on real (real estate) property, called ad valorem taxes. The county uses a formula to arrive at the amount of tax that is meant to make it fair to everyone.

The formula starts with the **fair market value (FMV)** of the property. This is theoretically the price the property would bring if placed on the market.

"Counties use various methods to determine the FMV. The process usually starts with, and sometimes ends with, comparables, or *comps* in real estate lingo. They compare a particular property with similar properties in the same neighborhood that have sold recently.

"If other three bedroom, three bath, two car garage houses of comparable age, construction and lot size are selling for $175,000, it is reasonable to assume that the property in question will command a similar price.

"Is this making sense so far?"

Allison asked, "You make it clear, but why is it necessary to know all this just to buy a Tax Lien Certificate?"

"Good question, actually there are four reasons:

- First of all you should never spend your money on anything you don't understand.

- Second, a little later on you may find yourself talking to property owners, Realtors or other investors. You need to know what they are talking about and you need to demonstrate that you know also.

- Also when you look at the property values on a list of Tax lien Certificates you need to know what you are seeing. Is this the Fair Market Value, or is it the assessed value and if it is the assessed value what percentage of the FMV does that represent.

- In addition, you are going to learn about more than just Tax Lien Certificates. That information will make more sense to you if you have some basic grounding in how real estate investing works.

"After determining the FMV, the county uses another formula to determine the *county constant.* The FMV is multiplied by the *county constant* to determine the *assessed value.*

"Okay, here is something you are going to hear me say often, "IT VARIES." It doesn't work exactly like this in every county, but it does in most. Just bear in mind that each state makes its' own rules, and sometimes so does each county in the state so be sure to check it out.

"The last step in the process is to take the total assessed value of all the properties in the county, and the amount of revenue needed by the county to arrive at a *mill (one tenth of a cent) levy.*

"The assessed value is multiplied by the mill levy and the product is the taxes that are assessed on the property. The County Tax Assessor sends the property owner a bill for this amount, with the expectation of prompt payment.

"In most cases taxes are paid promptly. A lot of property owners pay little attention to the entire process. If they financed the home the lender often takes care of the taxes from the escrow account set up at the time of the loan.

"As you would guess, the process is slightly more complicated but his will give you the basic understanding you need.

"There is one thing you need to understand before we go on. The values placed on the properties by the Assessors *tend* to be pretty conservative.

"The taxpayers themselves keep the values reasonable. If a taxpayer feels that their property has been overvalued and their taxes are too high they can appeal to the county. If they can offer evidence contrary to the assessed amount, the appraisal and assessed amount will be reduced.

"So here is how it works in real life. It is very simple. Let's use the $175,000 FMV house mentioned before. Assume the county constant is .09 and the mill levy is .12. The County Assessor will multiply the FMV of $175,000 by the .09 county constant and get an assessed value of $15,750. This is the amount you often see on the list of Tax Lien Certificates for sale.

"I saw a list on the internet before we came over here," Eric said. "I thought I was going to get a house for a few thousand dollars."

"That's why I am taking the time to go over this for you. A lot of people make the same mistake.

"If you know the county constant is .09 you can divide the $15,570 by .09 and know the FMV is $175,000. You are secured by $92 worth of real estate for every $1 you invest. Ask your broker or banker for that deal.

"Next the assessed value is multiplied by the .12 mill levy, and then lo and behold, this whole process ends with a tax assessment of $1,890."

"So if the taxpayer doesn't pay the tax bill the Tax Lien Certificate will be for $1,890, right?" Matt wanted to know.

"Well almost. The county may add some expenses on to the lien, but essentially you are correct," Lauren agreed.

"Wow, and this is a guaranteed investment, isn't it?" Eric was smiling.

"Allow me to clarify a point. If you go on the internet or listen to late night infomercials you will hear some of these promoters saying that Tax Lien Certificates are government guaranteed investments. That is misleading.

"The government doesn't guarantee the investment. The government guarantees the _rate of interest._ In other words, if the people pay their delinquent taxes they must also pay the interest and that rate is guaranteed to be 16% in Arizona. That is guaranteed. They will absolutely pay you 16% or they will lose their property to you. *It is not guaranteed that they will pay the taxes, or your interest.* But listen to this and see if you really care whether they pay or not.

"If they don't pay, this is where the security is important. If your $1,890 were invested in the stock market and it lost 10% what would you have?"

Aaron punched some numbers in his calculator and said, "$1,701."

"Right and what if real estate values fell by 10%. What would the value of the $175,000 house be in our example?"

Aaron punched the calculator again and said, "$157,000."

"Right. But what does that do to the value of your Tax Lien Certificate?"

Malone said, "For an instant it seemed that the value would decrease also, but now that I think about it, I am guessing it wouldn't be affected at all. Is that right?"

Lauren smiled, clapped her hands and said, "Right you are. The property owner still owes the same amount of taxes. Now that the value has decreased, the taxes may be lower next year, but that has no bearing on the Tax Lien Certificate that has been sold.

"The real estate is the security backing the value of the Tax Lien Certificate, so that is less. For example your $1,890 Tax Lien Certificate is now secured by $157,000 of real estate rather than $175,000.

"Are you particularly worried? No reason for worry at all. Even if the value declined 60%, which has happened in some areas of the country recently, you still are secured by $37 of real estate value for every $1 invested. Do you need to panic? Where else can you get this kind of security? Real estate values go up and down just like the stock market but I want my money in something that isn't affected by this roller coaster.

"Despite what you hear, investing in real estate carries many of the same risks as the stock market. Real estate values rarely fall to zero as we have some stocks do, but they do decrease; dramatically sometimes. I am going to teach you how to make money with real estate without ever owning real estate.

"Okay, we have covered why counties create Tax Lien Certificates. How they determine the amount of taxes to assess and how that determines the amount of the lien.

"I just don't believe you should put your money in anything you don't thoroughly understand. So does anyone have any questions?"

Eric said, "I think you have made it very easy to understand. I already know more about this than what is in my 401k, how about the rest of you?"

"I am anxious to know how we find these Tax Lien Certificates and how to evaluate them," Trish said.

"I know everyone is anxious but we aren't quite ready. You need to know that there are essentially three ways to buy Tax Lien Certificates:

1. First is at a live public auction. This is pretty much like any other auction and we will get into the details in a moment. Up until the last few years this was the way that all counties sold Tax Lien Certificates. Different counties set their own dates for auctions. Counties in Colorado hold auctions some time during the months of October, November and December. Different counties auction at different dates. All Arizona auctions were held on a specific date during the month of February. Many counties across the country still do it this way. But

more and more counties are going to our second method.....

2. Internet Auctions. This happens just as you would imagine, over the Internet. I will show you some screen shots of an actual auction where I bought almost $1,000,000 in Tax Lien Certificates in just three hours. This wasn't just a few really large liens there was around 250 of them in all denominations.

3. Assignment Purchases. This has been a favorite for many years. Quite often not all of the Certificates sell at the auction. These go back to the County or the state and they become the owner. In many counties you can just get a list of these liens, do your research and literally buy 'Over The Counter.'

"We have a lot to learn so let's learn how to buy at auctions first, and then we will move on to online auctions.

"If the taxes are not paid on the due date, you already know the taxes become a lien against the property" Lauren began.

"Then a penalty is assessed against the property. A Tax Lien Certificate is created and offered for sale at a public auction. The auction is open to anyone and is held in that county.

"Even though this a public auction, counties vary in the way they are conducted. Some still hold physical auctions that you must attend. However more and more counties hold their auctions on the Internet. I will explain both ways and both are very easy. I must admit that it is more fun, for most people, to go to a physical auction, but not as efficient. I think all counties will conduct their sales on the Internet soon so let's look at the physical auction first.

"This is where the investor comes into the picture. At the auction the certificate is sold according to the procedures established in that county. This is usually a *public auction* with oral bidding. Please keep in mind this is just one way to buy.

"You will find individuals with very limited funds, credit unions and banks with many thousands of dollars in surplus funds to invest at the same auction. Both have equal access, though not equal funds. Anyone can invest.

"About one month prior to the auction most counties prepare a list of all the properties that have delinquent taxes and will offer a Tax Lien Certificate for sale.

"The list of these properties is usually published in a newspaper of general circulation in that particular county four times in the month preceding the auction. It is not always the same newspaper each year. In some counties, newspapers bid on the job of publishing that list. Depending on the county, it can be several pages long.

"You can get on a list with the county to receive this section of the paper in the mail. Most counties charge a fee for the mailing. Counties with very large lists put these properties on a CD and you can purchase the list that way. For example Pima County Arizona will sell you the CD for $50.

"The county will furnish you with all the instructions for bidding either by mail or on the CD. Go to http://www.graham.az.gov/Graham_CMS/Treasurer for information on the Graham County, Arizona website. This is a county that still holds live auctions.

"You will need to register and furnish some information to the county on a form called a Buyer Data Form, or something similar. This has all your contact information, Social Security number – all the legal stuff you would expect.

"The payment methods vary by county also, as you have come to expect. For example most counties require payment by cash, cashier's check or money order. Still others will accept personal or business checks. Some require payment right at the time of purchase; some give you extra time, but usually just twenty-four hours.

"In most counties the investor gets a bidder card with a number on it after completing a Buyer Data Form. Most counties give you about the same kind of card you would get at an antique auction or a cattle auction.

"You will find that no matter who you are, or how much money you bring, if you want a seat you may need to get there early. These are public auctions, everyone has a chance.

"You will get an updated list of properties when you register. This list will have removed the names of all the taxpayers who have paid since the list was first published, during the previous month.

"Okay, let's take about a ten minute break. There are cold drinks and coffee in the back. Restrooms are down the hall on the right. Please be back in your seats in ten minutes. I think you have absorbed everything up to now, so after the break we will learn how to actually buy a Tax Lien Certificate at a public auction."

Chapter 4

THE PROTEGES LEARN THERE IS MORE THAN ONE WAY TO PARTICIPATE

"Don't wait till your ship comes in, swim out to it."

--Anonymous

"You know, I keep waiting for the other shoe to drop. This really sounds great, but what am I missing?" Trish asked the others while they were getting their drinks and stretching their legs.

Matt said, "I really don't think we are missing anything. I just think we don't know what we don't know yet. Both Kevin and Lauren said that these Tax Lien Certificates are the foundation to our financial house. Right now I think we are just getting the forms set and we are about to pour the concrete."

"Yeah, it is as though learning what a Tax Lien Certificate is and how they come into existence is the forms. Now we are going to learn how to bid at these auctions, so I am guessing that is the first load of cement to be poured." Eric looked a little puzzled but excited. "Anyway, our ten minutes is up so let's get back to our seats.

As soon as everyone was settled in, Lauren began, "I hope everyone found the facilities and have had some refreshments, so let's get right in to the process of actually buying a Tax Lien Certificate.

"I have told you that Tax Lien Certificates are sold at auctions; either live auctions or online auctions. We are going to start with live auctions. When when we get to the online auctions you will just have to see how the website works and you will be ready to go.

"First let's look at a list of liens available from Pinal County, Arizona." Lauren clicked the first slide on the TV monitor.

"Don't try to memorize anything on here. I just want you to have a look at what you would see on the county website. This is just one of many pages.

"First of all in the left column is the certificate number. This is an important number because it is used to look up individual liens. Let's look at the bottom listing number 101-16-10308. Next it shows the property owner's name and that taxes are past due for 2008 and 2009 as of the date of this list. The taxes are $268.56 the county has fees or interest due in the amount of $36.64 and the total is $305.20.

"So Aaron, how much will the Tax Lien Certificate cost?"

"$305.20, if I understand this."

"You understand perfectly. If you go to the top of the page you will see the first lien listed is for over $2,888. So you see just on this one page there is a real difference in the amount you need to invest. I just want you to see how the information will come to you. We will delve deeply into similar lists as we go on."

Eric asked, "Do you mean that all this information is available on this individual, and we are looking at it without his permission."

"It is all a matter of public record and a little later on you will see how much more information is available. This isn't an invasion of privacy, this is information that is necessary in order to conduct business in a real estate market. So let's move on.

"Okay, we are at the auction and you are ready to bid. How do you do it?" Eric and Matt both smiled. "You are ahead of me. You guessed it; there is more than one way.

"For example if this was a sale in Colorado the bidding would start at the $305.20, in our example and then you would bid on how much you would be willing to pay for this certificate.

"Since the information on the screen is from Arizona, where the interest rate is 16% the successful bidder is the one that will accept the lowest rate of interest. For example the bidding will open at 16%; the first bid may be for 15.75%. Someone else may bid 15.5% and if no one else bids he will purchase the certificate and it will earn him 15.5% until it is paid off or if it isn't in three years he can own the property."

"Whoa, whoa, whoa," Malone was frowning. "I thought you said the rate in Arizona is set by law and can't go down, now here is someone buying the lien and it pays 15.5%. What gives?"

"The state does guarantee the 16% rate but you may be willing to accept less in order to get the lien. Remember, this is an auction. Now, walk with me very carefully here. Stop me on any point that is confusing. The only dumb question is the one not asked. So don't be embarrassed if you don't understand a point.

"Don't start thinking that you can't get the very highest rate. At the 2010 sale, which is where this screen shot came from, 35% of the liens went for the full 16% and 50% were higher than 15%.

"As we get further into this you will learn to buy all your liens at the maximum rate. Right now we are just talking about the public auction.

"Does this make you feel better Malone?"

"Somewhat, it just startled me at first."

"I understand, we have to give this to you in blocks of information, otherwise you would be completely overwhelmed."

At this point Lauren went on to explain that there are actually three ways to bid.

BIDDING PROCEDURE NUMBER 1

You **bid down** the interest rate. As in the example that Lauren gave Malone, the successful bidder is the one that will accept the lowest interest rate. She also explained that *Couch buyers can always get the maximum rate!*

BIDDING PROCEDURE NUMBER 2

Some states, Colorado for example, has **premium bidding**; also known as **bidding up.** The rate of interest remains constant but the certificate is sold to the buyer who pays the largest amount in excess of the taxes, penalty interest, advertising and any other charges provided by law. The premium is not returned to the investor in Colorado but is returned in some other states.

BIDDING PROCEDURE NUMBER 3

In this procedure, the competitive bidding is for whoever is willing to accept the smallest **undivided interest** in the property in the event of foreclosure. Remember, they are rarely foreclosed. Iowa is an undivided interest state, so you collect the full 24% interest rate. If you bid the property down to 50%, for example, and you foreclose you would own 50% of the property.

People often get hung up on these foreclosure procedures. Don't. There are two things you should keep in mind.

- The amount you pay for a Tax Lien Certificate is very small in relation to the property value. So even 50% of the property is still a great deal.

- You are still making 24% and your money will double every three years!

The following table will give you the information that Lauren gave to the protégés as a hand-out.

Bidding Procedures by State

Alabama – 12%

Alabama is a *bid up* state. You bid on the total amount due and the successful bidder is the one who bids the most over the amount due. Alabama is one of those states where the surplus bid goes back to the bidder at redemption, unlike Colorado.

Arizona – 16%

In Arizona you *bid down* the interest rate and the bidder willing to accept the lowest rate is the successful buyer.

Colorado – 9% Plus the Federal Discount Rate

The interest rate is 9% plus whatever the Federal Discount is on September first preceding the auctions that take place in October, November and December. Colorado is a *bid up* state. Investors bid up the amount to pay over the total amount of taxes and expenses due. The largest premium bidder is the buyer. The county keeps the surplus and the property owner pays no interest on the surplus.

Florida – 18%

In Florida you **bid down** the interest rate and the one willing to accept the lowest rate of interest is the buyer.

Georgia – 20%

Technically Georgia is not a Tax Lien Certificate state. Auctions are held just as in a Tax Lien Certificate auction. The successful bidder receives an actual deed to the property. However it is a "Restricted Deed." The deed is restricted for one year. During this one year the property owner can redeem the deed by paying all penalties and interest. If not redeemed the deed becomes an absolute deed at the end of one year.

Georgia is a **bid up** state. If the property is redeemed the investor gets the bid-up premium refunded by the county. The property owner pays interest on the surplus. In the event of foreclosure the county keeps the surplus.

*There are ways the investor can earn more than 20%. Lauren explains later.

Illinois -- 18% for first six months then doubles to 36%

Illinois is a **bid down** state. Peculiarities in Illinois are discussed later.

Indiana -- 10% first 6 months, 15% for the next 6 months, 25% in subsequent years.

Indiana is a *bid up* state. Property owners pay interest on the surplus. Surplus goes to investor at redemption. It is kept by the county if foreclosed.

Iowa – 24%

Iowa is a state where you bid on an ***undivided interest.*** The successful bidder is the one who accepts the smallest percentage of undivided interest in the property. You become a joint owner with the delinquent taxpayer/owner.

Kentucky – 12%

Kentucky presents still another way to bid. Their Tax Lien Certificates are sold by *lottery.* If more than one person wants to buy a lien there is a lottery held on the spot to select the buyer.

Louisiana – 1% per month, plus 5% penalty

Louisiana is another state where you bid on an ***undivided interest.***

Maryland – Varies by county and some cities 12% to 24%

A *bid up* state. One quirk; the excess bid is sold on credit, if you want.

Missouri – 10%

Missouri is a *bid up* state. Surplus goes back to investor if redeemed

Nebraska – 14%

Nebraska is an *undivided interest* state

New Hampshire – 18%

New Hampshire is an *undivided interest* state.

New Jersey -- 18%

New Jersey is a *bid down* state. The rate starts at 18% but can go up

New York – 18%

Check individual counties. New York is a challenge.

North Dakota -- 12%

North Dakota is a *bid down* state.

Oklahoma – 8%

Oklahoma is another *lottery* state.

South Dakota – 12%

South Dakota is a *bid down* state.

West Virginia – 12%

West Virginia is a *bid up* state. The surplus goes to the investor at redemption, but the surplus does not earn interest.

Lauren said, "This hand-out does not include all the states. It is meant to just give you a good sampling. You need to look up all the information for yourself on any state where you want to buy Tax Lien Certificates. If I gave you every piece of information on each state, the sheet I gave could actually go to several volumes. But don't let the amount of information available intimidate you. You will never invest in all 3,000 counties. Find three or four counties in each state you like and become an expert on those counties.

"Remember, I have already shown you how buying "over-the-counter" may be your very best strategy. Maximum interest and no competition are huge pluses."

Allison asked, "This is so amazing, but I keep having this nagging feeling that there must be a downside to all this, is there one?"

"There is a downside to everything," Lauren answered. "However the only downside is a lack of education. If you learn the simple lessons I am sharing, you have the safest investment in existence.

"Here is an example of how an uneducated person can incur a serious downside. If you look at your handout you will see that Colorado is a *premium bid* state. The Tax Lien Certificate will go to the investor willing to pay the largest premium over the amount of taxes.

"Follow me carefully on this, I will show you how a premium bid can be bad or great. Let's assume that you find a Tax Lien Certificate that you want that is listed for $1,000. At the auction other investors are also interested in this certificate and start bidding up the premium. Finally the successful bid is $1,200. The premium is $200.

"As you see the rate in Colorado is 9% plus the Federal Discount Rate on the first day of September preceding the

Tax Lien Certificate auction. For our illustration let's assume the Federal Discount Rate was 4%; this makes the Colorado rate 13%.

"Now we own a certificate that carries a guaranteed rate of interest of 13%. But do we actually earn 13%? Think about it. The taxpayer pays 13% if they redeem the Certificate on the amount of taxes due; 13% X $1,000, or $130. But we paid, not $1,000, we paid $1,200, so $130 is 10.85% of our $1,200 investment.

"If the property owner redeems after one year this is our yield. What if he redeems the day after the auction? How much does he owe, Aaron?"

"Well he would only owe the $1,000 plus interest for only one day, if I am following you correctly," Aaron answered.

"You are following correctly," Lauren smiled. "So we get back our $1,000 plus some small change and we just lost $200."

Eric said, "So this is the type of thing to watch out for and why we need some education before we start investing. The lesson I am getting is to just never invest in a state that has premium bidding. So why would anyone invest in Colorado?"

"This is where a lot of research is needed. If you find reason to believe that the property owner will not redeem you stand the chance of picking up some very prime property.

"Do you remember when we were learning to research in Pinal County? One of the first things I asked you to look for on the Assessor's website was the address of the property owner and compare it to the address of the property? If the property owner lives in another state, it sometimes means they have moved from the state and have actually abandoned the property? How might we find out, Matt?"

"I'm not sure, but the first thing that comes to mind is to try and find a phone listing for the owner at the out of state address."

"Right you are. You could also mail a registered letter, return receipt requested and see if it is deliverable. Lots of ways, but if the letter comes back it means that the tax notice from the county has probably been returned also, so the owner may not even be aware that taxes are due. For a great property it would be worth some effort.

"Eric, you said that you just wouldn't invest in a state with premium bidding. I'm guessing that you might not want to go through this hassle, right?"

"Yeah, with so many certificates available why go through the brain damage?"

"Here comes that education thing again. Sometimes you may want to pay a premium and as much as possible."

"From the Cheshire Cat smile you are wearing, I am guessing there is more to this story, right?" Trish asked.

Lauren laughed, "I warned you that there were lots of variables and here is a great one.

"Premium bidding doesn't always work the way it does in Colorado. Sometimes it is a very good thing. There are states where the surplus earns interest and the surplus goes back to the investor if the property is redeemed. You will find some of those states in the samples I gave you on the handout.

"Let's look at Georgia. As you see Georgia is not technically a Tax Lien Certificate state, but their restricted deeds acts just like a Tax Lien Certificate. Even though you receive a deed at the auction, the property owner still has one year to redeem the property. Georgia assesses a 20% penalty, ***not interest***, during this period.

"Now what is the difference in the *penalty* paid in Georgia, as opposed to *interest* paid in most states? I won't make you guess. The penalty is due immediately, so if the property owner redeems the day after the auction the full 20% must be paid. Remember in our Colorado example the interest for one day was very small but if it had been a penalty the full 13% would have to be paid making the investment much more lucrative.

"There are a couple more differences. As you will recall we have talked about the fact that the property owner pays delinquent taxes to the county and the county pays the investor. In Georgia the property owner must pay the investor the full amount that the investor paid the county.

This includes taxes, 20% penalty, expenses *and the premium paid by the investor.*

"Consider what happens to an investor who is bidding on a $5,000 deed and has to bid $3,000 more because of the competition. We will assume that the investor redeems very soon, say one week, after the auction. If this happened in Colorado we have already learned that the investor will lose $3,000.

"It is much different in Georgia and some other premium bid states."

Lauren gave everyone another handout showing what would happen.

GEORGIA PREMIUM BID EXAMPLE

The owner owes $5,000 in taxes and redeems the tax deed one week after the auction.

The total taxes due from the owner
$5,000

The penalty rate is 20% so owner pays another
$1,000

The investor paid $3,000 premium so owner also owes

20% penalty on premium $ 600

TOTAL DUE FROM PROPERTY OWNER
$6,600

The investor gets his $5,000 back, plus 20% X $5,000, or $1,000 in penalty on taxes plus 20% X $3,000 penalty on premium then the county refunds the $3,000 premium to the investor.

TOTAL BACK TO INVESTOR $9,600
■■ ■ ■ ■

These figures would be true if the owner redeems anytime during the first twelve months. At the end of twelve months the property can be claimed by the investor.

Lauren said, "There is one caveat; if the owner doesn't redeem the county retains the surplus. Of course, the investor has the property so it isn't a terrible blow. Also, in most places the owner can recover the $3,000 premium from the county, but that is another subject.

"We have talked a lot about research, so how do we do it?"

Chapter 5

PEEK BEHIND THE CURTAIN

How you do anything, is how you do everything.

---Anonymous

"I think the easiest way to understand research is to use a live example. Do you remember the web address I gave you when we met at Kevin and Dagney's house?"

Not everyone raised their hand. "Let's walk through this so we all understand. To remind you, the web address was www.wowworks.com. This is where we start if we don't already have a specific address."

Lauren had a large screen TV set up with a computer hook-up. She clicked and the screen shot of www.Wowworks.com *(Illustration 1)* came up. "We have talked a lot about Arizona, so let's just stick with that. If you look over here on the left side of the screen you will see a list of states. So let's click on Arizona.

Illustration 1

"Now here *(Illustration 2)* on the left is what we are looking for. You see there is a list of counties. I know Kevin and Dagney have bought a lot of Tax Lien Certificates in Pinal County. Dagney's dad lives in Tucson, which is in Pima County just south of Pinal County that makes it handy for them to own property there. You will learn just how handy a little later. Look down under ARIZONA for *County Web Sites*. So let's click on Pinal County.

Illustration 2

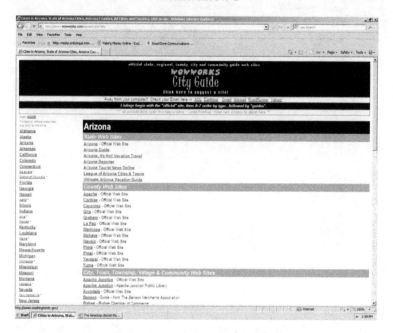

"When we get the Pinal County home page we want to look under: "Elected Officials" and find –"Treasurer." In most counties Tax Lien Certificate sales are handled by the Treasurer, however in some states they are handled by the "Tax Collector."

After we get to the "Treasurer" page you will find a box on the left that says, "Tax Lien Searches," Illustration 3 shows what we will see.

Illustration 3

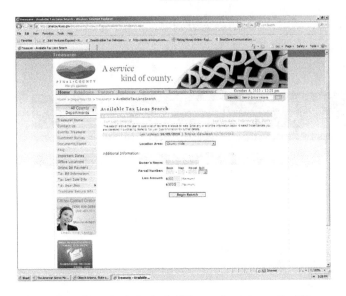

"The first box is labeled, "Location Area." We can search the entire county or click at the end of this box for a dropdown box. This will show the different towns in the county. For our purpose today, we want our search to include the entire county.

"Then you will see that you can enter an owner's name or parcel number and search for an individual property.

"We are going down to the next boxes and search for "Lien Amounts." I have entered $300 to $3,000. Searches can be for any amounts. We click for the search and Illustration four will show the first page of available liens.

Illustration 4

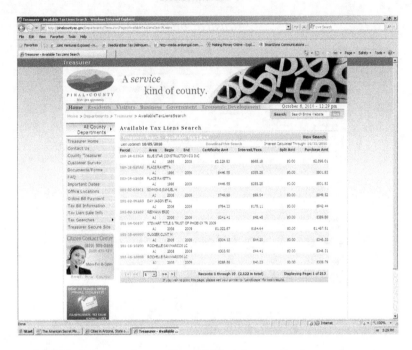

"The left column shows Parcel Numbers. Let's go down to 101-10-09907. The owner's name is in the left column. Remember, we are not violating anyone's privacy. These are public records. Even though this shows there are taxes due, that does not comment on the owner's character. There are hundreds of reasons why there are taxes due. So don't form any opinions from this information. With that said, let's click on this parcel number.

Illustration 5

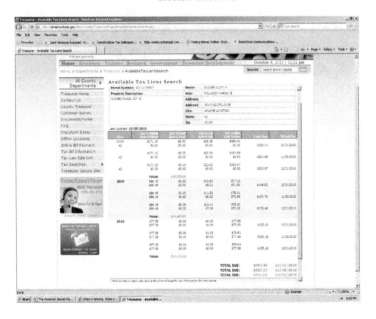

"You can see that taxes for 2008, 2009 and so far 2010 are unpaid. At the bottom of the page we see that amount due if paid by different dates.

"Here is a bit of information that I want you to think about. Here we are in October of 2010. Tax sales in Arizona are held in February. So the sale is over and yet here are Tax Lien Certificates for sale. As a matter of fact, if you look at the bottom of the page, you will see there are 2,117 certificates unsold. Hhmmm!!

"Malone, remember how concerned you were with getting the full 16% interest rate?

"Yes, that still troubles me a little."

"I can see that, so let's go to our drop box on the left and click on *Tax Lien Sale Info*. You see some PDF downloads at the top of the page.

Illustration 6

Let's click on *Information Booklet*. Then let's go to page 3 and look down about the middle of the page until you see this------

Tax liens not sold at the tax lien sale will be offered and may be purchased at the full rate of 16% when the Treasurer has processed all successful bids. This could be up to three days after the auction. Tax liens sold after the Tax Lien Sale are sold on a first come, first served basis.

"Here we are eight months after the sale and we have our choice of over 2,000 liens for sale over-the-counter at the full 16%. Also, *NO BIDDING!!!* This is called an **ASSIGNMENT PURCHASE.**

"Some counties have hundreds, even thousands, of liens that were not purchased at the auction. There are great opportunities in these **ASSIGNMENT PURCHASES**, as you are about to see. But caution is the watchword. You need to carefully research these liens. Most of the time these liens were not sold at auction because the investors thought that the property was not worth the amount they would have to pay for the lien.

"That certainly isn't always true. We just looked at one of these parcels that is available for sale for a little over $500. Let's look at that property a little closer and see if it is junk, as some of the late night gurus and other so-called **"EXPERTS"** tell us.

"Let's go to the *Assessor* website. Look on the left for *'Parcel Search.'* You will see that I have already entered our parcel number 101-10-09907. It doesn't exactly fit in the boxes.

Illustration 7

"Here is the information we are looking for from the *Assessor's* website.

Illustration 8

"Now, you will start to learn why I spent time talking about FMV, Assessed Value etc. You will see, at the bottom left that the FCV, the county's idea of the Fair Market Value, and is $13,581. We apply the 10% ratio and find that the assessed FCV is $1,358. Their county constant and mill levy will be applied to this number to determine the taxes for the year.

"Right now we are more interested in the box on the right. The first thing we want to check is the *Billing Address* and the *Property Address*. They are the same on this property which tells us that the owner probably lives on the property.

"If the owner's address was different it would indicate an absentee owner. More about how important this is later.

"Look right below the *Property Address* and we will click on *View Map*.

Page | 102

Illustration 9

"We were offered several views; we chose the satellite view. You can zoom in or out for the clearest view, but you are still looking straight down. So let's take the little man icon at the top of the zoom control, click on him, drag him over the balloon 'A,' which indicates our property and we will get a view from the street.

"A word of caution here. The balloon is not always entirely accurate so if you are buying the property check it out.

Illustration 10

Here is the property that has a Tax Lien Certificate available, over-the-counter, for a little over $500 that carries a full 16% rate of interest. So do you think you would be well secured?

"This is like shopping for guaranteed interest rate investments from Wal-Mart. You just shop till you find something that appeals to you, is in your price range and you buy it. You will either earn 16% interest, or you will own the property. No genius ability required.

"If you are going to an auction, or plan to buy online, you will want to get on the county list to be notified in advance of the sale date. *Illustration 11* shows a typical notice. This is one I receive every year from Colorado.

Illustration 11

To our tax certificate investors,

The Colorado tax certificate auctions are opening. The website locations, start dates, and end dates follow. We hope to see you there and wish for your success.

County	URL
Start	End
Adams County	https://www.adamstaxsale.com
Tue 10/12/2010	Fri 11/05/2010
Arapahoe County	https://www.arapahoetaxsale.com
Fri 10/15/2010	Mon 11/08/2010
Archuleta County	https://www.archuletataxsale.com
Tue 10/12/2010	Thu 11/04/2010
Denver County	https://www.denvertaxsale.com
Mon 10/18/10	Fri 11/05/2010
Grand County	https://www.grandtaxsale.com
Fri 10/01/10	Thu 11/04/2010
Weld County	https://www.weldtaxsale.com
Mon 10/4/2010	Mon 11/01/2010

"Let's talk about investing online."

Chapter 6

HOW TO BEAT THE PANTS OFF THE BEST WALL STREET GURU, AND NEVER GET OFF YOUR COUCH

"An investment in knowledge always pays the best interest."

-Benjamin Franklin

Each year more and more counties are going to online auctions. This makes it easier to keep all your Tax Lien Certificate money working all the time. As a Tax Lien Certificate is redeemed and you receive your money, you will want to re-invest again right away so the money keeps earning for you.

You can often find another sale in some other state, check Florida, or just make an *ASSIGNMENT PURCHASE.*

Recently I was challenged by one of the "I know everything and you know nothing" gurus.

I was explaining how to amass a fortune in Tax Lien Certificates. This *genius?* was quick to point out that as you accumulate a lot of money, Tax Liens would be getting paid off and it would become a full time job to keep the money invested.

In the last chapter Lauren showed her protégés how easy it is to buy *'over-the-counter.'* There were over 2,000 liens available and she showed how ten minutes of work uncovered a great lien that earns the full 16% rate of interest allowed in Arizona.

As this is being written in November, 2010, there is something else at work that is going to change the game for the next several years. In all my books, seminars, radio programs and various training courses, I have always pointed out that an investor only gets the property about 3% of the time. Historically, this has been correct. So if you bought one hundred Tax Lien Certificates, you had a good chance of having three of those liens actually resulting in the investor getting the property.

Barb and I have not had that experience. We have never gotten the deed from an investment in a Tax Lien Certificate. Of course 3% is an average. It didn't apply to every one hundred investments. You might buy one thousand liens without a single one going to deed and get ten out of the next one hundred.

The ruin of our real estate market by the Federal Government has completely skewed the numbers. People with great credit are walking away from their homes and allowing them to be foreclosed because they aren't worth what they owe, and won't be worth that much in the foreseeable future.

Here is what is happening now from personal experience.

A little over four years ago a wealthy friend of ours asked us to invest one million dollars for him in Tax Lien Certificates. He wanted to do it right away and he wanted to buy a lot of liens.

We all agreed that Phoenix, in Maricopa County, AZ, was a great place to buy at the time. It was right at the end of the year when he asked us to do this for him. That didn't give us much time since the Arizona sales are always in February, just two months away. Phoenix sales are held online.

Our friend wanted to be a successful bidder on lots of properties so he wanted us to bid 7%. I tried to persuade him to go higher, but he was interested in getting lots of liens with the expectation that several would go to deed.

We cautioned him that at a 3% average, he might be looking at six deeds; or none. He was adamant, and as you will see, he was entirely correct.

Barb and I spent a few hours per day for less than a week and identified over two hundred properties to bid on. So much for this turning into a full time job, but if it did turn into a full time job, how bad would that be?

On the day of the sale we were successful bidders on over two hundred liens.

In Arizona a property has a three year redemption period and they can redeem the lien at any time during the redemption period. Our investor would still have an excellent investment that earned 7%.

The market was starting down at the time of the auction. As we all know it has crashed in the last three years right along with employment. As a result, he did much better than the 3%.

We bid on 302 properties for a total bid of $1,291,180. We were outbid on some of our bids but we wound up with 223 properties for a price of $948,825.

Here in *Illustration 12* is a screen shot of the actual bid summary.

Illustration 12

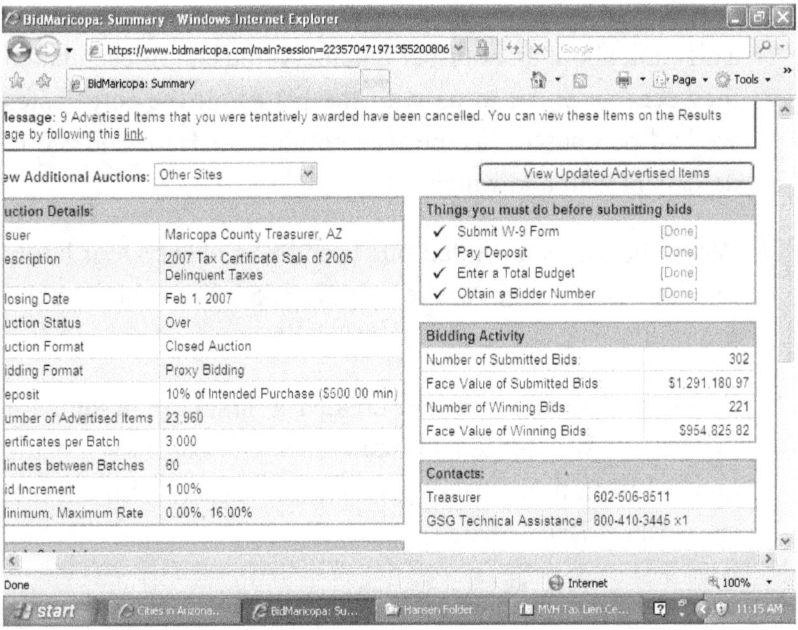

You will see on the top right side the things that had to be done before the auction. Among the four items is "Enter a Total Budget," that was $1,000,000. Our friend had to post a deposit of $100,000 and submit a W-9 IRS form. The company handling the sale sent us the "Bidder Number."

You will see on the left that there were 23,960 Tax Lien Certificates in the auction. All this was handled by computer. We had the login to access all 23,960 Tax Lien Certificates. We picked out the 302 that we want to bid on and submitted them to the auction company.

The computer looked at 3,000 liens in each batch; so there were 9 batches. The computer scanned the first batch, identified the ones we bid on and awarded them to us if no one else had agreed to accept less than 7%.

This took about an hour per batch. At the end of each batch they sent an email to us with the list of all the certificates we had purchased. There was nothing for Barb and me to do except wait and watch.

When the sale was ended our friend had twenty-four hours to wire transfer them the remaining $854,825, which he did promptly.

Before the auction we had created a Tracking system for the liens. We needed to keep track of seasoning on the liens. Illustration 13 will give you a snapshot of the Excel spreadsheet Barb created.

You can get a copy for your use at no charge by requesting it from Barb at barbyocom@comcast.net.

Illustration 13

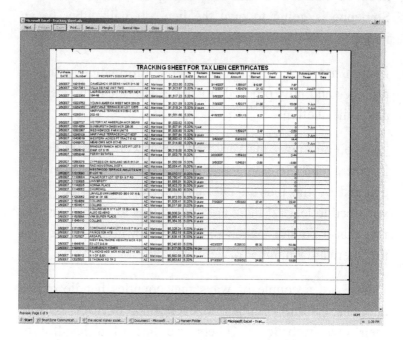

I haven't seen his final tally, but the last time I checked there was more than 50 properties ready for him to foreclose.

There are a couple of things at work now.

1. A lot more people are unable to pay their taxes or continue monthly payments if the property is financed.

2. There are fewer people who can afford to buy the properties.

I certainly don't mean to make light of the situation where so many of our citizens find themselves these days. But

Page | 111

keep in mind you are not taking advantage of them. Someone is going to own the lien. It will either be an investor or the county or state.

Lauren has covered all this general information with her protégés and now proceeds to share with them the steps to an online auction.

"As you all know, the very first things you need to decide is where you are going to invest. Probably this will be dictated by the interest rate and redemption period. Then you need to learn if there are lots of liens available, just the fact that a county has an online auction gives you a clue that there are a number of liens available.

"There are a couple of ways that counties handle online auctions. Some counties do everything themselves from their own websites. Others use one of a handful of companies that handle everything for the county.

"You can learn their procedures from links on the county website.

"Let's look at Maricopa County Arizona. They have historically had thousands of liens available. They also contract a commercial company, THE GRANT STREET GROUP. This company handles their sales and also sales for other counties in other states.

"In the upper right corner of the Maricopa County Treasurer's website at http://treasurer.maricopa.gov/research/tutorial/tutorial.htm we find several bullet points. One is called "Bidder

Application *(PDF)."* You will need to go to that page and complete the application to obtain a user name and password. Then you can go to www.bidmaricopa.com. Here is what you will see.......

Illustration 14

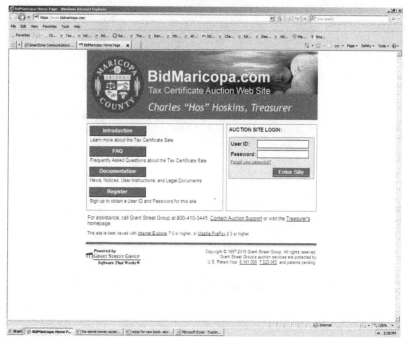

"Once you have your name and password go to the AUCTION SITE LOGIN.

"There are no sales today so the only thing you will see is information on previous sales. The most important thing to check out now is the Auction Demo and Trial Auction. Once you have gone through these tutorials, you are ready for the auction.

Illustration15

"You have had a look at how both a physical auction and an online auction works. As you have seen neither is complicated.

"There is one other thing to be aware of while you are doing your research. There may be liens other than the Tax Lien Certificates. If you are buying liens on improved real estate; in other words there is a house or commercial building on the property, the owner may have mortgaged the property and the lender will have filed a lien or Trust Deed.

"If this is the situation, you are almost assured that the lien will be paid off and you will not get the property but get whatever rate of interest you have accepted. If the owner does not redeem the Tax Lien Certificate during the redemption period you may now apply for a deed.

"As you would expect different states handle the deed process in different ways. For example;

- **Colorado** You apply for a Treasurer's Deed from the County Treasurer

- **Arizona** You have two ways to go, Here is the first from the County Website

Deeding Process: In order for you to obtain a deed to the property purchased by a tax lien, you must hold a tax lien certificate for three (3) years from the date the certificate was offered for sale, then bring a foreclosure action in a court of competent jurisdiction within Pinal County to foreclose on your lien (ARS 42-18203/18204).

"Since the redemption period is three years, you are able to start foreclosure immediately. You can also just hold the lien for five years and receive the deed without foreclosure.

- **Florida** Florida has still another way to obtain the deed. At the end of the two year redemption period the certificate owner can apply to the county for a deed and the county will conduct an auction of the certificate and the winner of the auction will receive a deed. If the certificate owner wants the property they get first bid. The certificate owner will bid enough to get back his/her investment plus expenses and however much more they want to bid. They will either get the property or at least make a nice profit.

"Liens can be filed for other reasons also. If a person has been sued successfully the person bringing the suit can record their judgment and this can become a lien on everything the property owner owns.

"There can also be IRS and State liens. Sometimes there are liens placed by cities because the owner didn't keep the weeds mowed on vacant lots. The list is almost endless.

Aaron had a puzzled look, "With the possibility of all these liens, how can we ever be safe if we take title to the property?"

"Well, you can know in advance." Lauren said. "You can check this information online in most counties. Incidentally I don't recommend buying in a county that does not have a good searchable website unless you live in the county.

"In most counties you can go to the County Clerk page, some counties call it the County Recorder, and enter the owner's name and find every legal action that has ever been recorded about them.

"Sometimes you find some surprises there. For instance you may learn that the owner has recently filed for bankruptcy protection. That isn't a caution; it is a red light, at least until the bankruptcy has been dismissed.

"Federal tax liens are another caution. These and state liens are the only liens superior to a Tax Lien in most states, but there are exceptions so check it out. If you find something recorded that you don't understand call the County Clerk/Tax Collector and quiz them at length.

"There is a bright light. Most liens are wiped out by foreclosing on the Tax Lien Certificate, which is superior to all except Federal liens, in most states. So even if there is a mortgage loan on the property, it will be wiped out.

"As we get into my recommendations for your financial planning I am going to make some recommendations that make most of these issues irrelevant.

"For example, Kevin divides his investments in categories. At the foundation is Tax Lien Certificates. He invests in tax liens strictly for the high rate of interest. Because of the way he invests, his liens get paid off sometime during the redemption period. He is assured that almost all of his liens will be paid off because he only invests in established residential neighborhood.

"He doesn't do a lot of research. All the problems I am warning you about only apply in that 1% or 2% of the cases where you actually acquire the property. An even smaller percentage of the 1% or 2% will have a problem.

"Here is another caveat, *"Don't put all your eggs in one basket."* Kevin takes this very seriously. For example he doesn't like the large dollar amount of liens. He feels that if he is going to invest $10,000 he would prefer to have 5 liens for $2,000 each.

"He isn't concerned about losing his money. His concern is that the liens get paid off at different times. While he is making arrangements to put the money he just received from a payoff back to work, the other liens are still earning interest.

"Trish, at the last break you were talking about the lack of liquidity in Tax Lien Certificates."

"Yes, I was. But with your explanation I view it as much less a problem," Trish said.

Lauren nodded her head, "Yes, you know the maximum amount of time you might hold a Tax Lien certificate before you collect your money or the property.

Knowing this, you do not invest dollars that you may need for an emergency.

"Tax Lien Certificates are assignable and can be bought and sold. Don't rely on this if you need immediate cash. There are a handful of companies that will market you liens for you for a fee. I am not going to name them because I can't vouch for their integrity.

"The buyers of Tax Lien Certificates are a matter of public record. You can get a list of these buyers and offer them your lien if you are in a hurry. Be prepared to have to discount the certificate if you need an immediate sale.

"This is a wealth-building vehicle, not a trading vehicle. The lack of liquidity is one of the best reasons to invest in Tax Lien Certificates. Since you know you can't get your money out quickly you look elsewhere for ready cash. Your money is still working for you long after most emergencies have come and gone.

"Now everyone take about a ten minute break and then we will talk about Tax Deeds. When we finish with that we will break for lunch. I will have a special surprise for you right after lunch."

Chapter 7

SO YOU WANT SOME PROPERTY?

Any intelligent fool can make things bigger and more complex. It takes a touch of genius – and a lot of courage to move in the opposite direction.

- *Albert Einstein*

"Okay, is everyone ready to go a little longer before lunch?" Lauren asked.

"We are going to talk about Tax Deeds. You have already learned much of what you need to know in order to buy a Tax Deed.

"Remember we learned that over thirty states sell Tax Lien Certificates and the remainder of the states sell Tax Deeds – Tax Lien Certificates do not give you title to the property unless it is not redeemed during the redemption period. On the other hand a Tax Deed gives you title to property. In some states you get title right away, and as you have come to expect others have different procedures to go through before you actually obtain the deed. We will talk about some of these differences."

Matt raised his hand, "May I ask a question before we get started?"

"Of course. Don't let me leave one subject before you have all your questions answered. What do you want to ask, Matt?"

"I understand how someone can get behind on their taxes, but I can't believe that very many people ever get far enough behind that the county actually auctions off their property. How does this happen?"

"Matt, that is a great question and there as many reasons as there are properties. For example:

- **DEATH** – Of course most property passes to heirs upon the death of the owner, but some people have no relatives, or at least none that can be found so the property just passes to the county.

- **JAIL** – A certain number of property owners go to jail and can't deal with their property and some even die there.

- **HARD TIMES** – Many people fall on hard times and just get to the point where they can't think clearly. They assume that they are going to lose the property anyway and they just abandon it.

- **WORTHLESS PROPERTY** – Some property just becomes worth less than the taxes and the owners just walk away.

"Sometimes people just get careless. Here is a great example.

Lauren smiled and without saying a word handed a reprint from an article in *The Miami Herald* to everyone.

(See Appendix for readable text)

"I could go on, but I think you get the picture. Not only are there lots of reasons why people give up their property, there are lots of ways to acquire Tax Deeds. I just kind of lump them all together and call them 'Tax Defaulted Investment Opportunities.'

"First of all there are just outright Tax Deed auctions. These auctions are just the same as a Tax Lien Certificate auction except that you are actually buying the property.

"You can obtain a tax deed to a property in some states through what they call a *NEGOTIATED LIST*. This is a list of properties that have not sold in previous sales, have been deeded to the state and can be bought directly with no minimum purchase amount."

"Did you say there is no minimum bid? Does that mean I could bid $10," Trish wanted to know.

"That's right," Lauren answered. "That doesn't mean that the state will accept the offer that is why it is called a negotiated list. If they don't accept your offer, they sometimes counter your offer but not always. In any case if they don't accept your first offer you can submit another offer for a different amount."

Lauren clicked the screen again and *Illustration 15* came up. "This is a page from the Land Commissioner of Arkansas website, the URL is www.cosl.org. This has been a great state to buy land in the past. You will see that state owned land is divided into three categories; S2, S3 and S4. These categories indicate how long the state has had the real estate for sale. S4 is the category where you can bid any amount. As you can see you can get the lists in either Excel or PDF Format."

Illustration 15

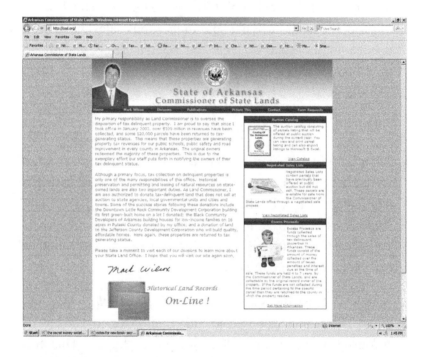

"You have come to expect that different states handle their sales differently. Not only are the sales procedures different, the deed process is different. Let's look at two states that offer exceptional opportunities; Texas and Georgia.

"The opportunities are exceptional, but they have some hoops to jump through. Let's start with Georgia.

"Georgia Tax Deed auctions are similar to any other real estate auction. The bidding starts at the amount of taxes and expenses due and the property is sold to the highest bidder. In almost all cases the successful bid is for some amount over the amount due the county.

"This *premium bid* is unlike the premium bidding you learned about in Colorado Tax Lien Certificate auctions. As you will recall, in Colorado when the property owner redeems the property you receive your investment plus the interest earned but the premium amount is not returned to you.

"Even though we are talking about a Tax Deed rather than a Tax Lien Certificate, there are definite similarities in Georgia.

"For example there is a one year redemption period, and a PENALTY, not interest rate of 20%. So if the property owner redeems the property during the one year period, he must pay everything that you bid, *including the premium,* plus 20%. So not only do you get back the premium you bid, but you also collect a 20% penalty also.

"There is another advantage to investing in Georgia; there are Tax Deed sales monthly. So if one of your deeds redeems early you can re-invest quickly to keep your money working.

"As you expect there is also a negative – you must be present at the auction or hire someone to attend and bid on your behalf. This can get expensive.

"There are several things to be especially careful about at the end of the year when you start to foreclose on your deed. They are too lengthy to try and explain here so you want to do a lot of research, or hire a local attorney well versed in the procedures.

"My advice is to make sure there is a sizeable profit potential in any real estate you obtain in Georgia because the expenses can be sizeable. Kevin only bids on property that he is very sure will be redeemed. For example, it could be someone's residence. They will rarely lose their property for the amount of taxes due.

"Kevin knows that regardless of the amount of his bid he will recoup the total amount, plus his expenses and a full 20% penalty. If the property owner redeems the first month he has an annualized yield of 240%.

Matt still looked puzzled, "All this just blows my mind. With all these opportunities you would think everyone would know about them."

"Before Kevin began to tell you about these opportunities, did you know about them?" Lauren asked.

"No, you are right I didn't, but it just seems to me that the only properties that you could buy this way would just be pretty much worthless."

Lauren smiled and reminded them of the reprint from an article in *The Miami Herald* she had given to everyone as she clicked the next illustration.....

Illustration 16

From the *Florida Times Union*

Jacksonville taxpayers foot the bill for $86,000 investor profit on Shipyards tax lien

Posted: May 18, 2010 - 5:36pm

When the developers of the twice-failed Shipyards project didn't pay their 2008 property taxes, two out-of-town investors were happy to pick up the tab — with 17 percent interest and an outside chance at getting the land.

Now, Jacksonville taxpayers will foot the bill for the investors' tidy profit of $86,000 — enough to pay for two of the 40-plus Jacksonville city employees who'll be pink-slipped this summer.----------

--- Clogging that title are the two investors, who will have liens on the property if the taxes aren't paid. And every month, the payoff for the city — and profit for the investors — inches up another 17 percent.

---- One of the buyers is listed as Pender Newkirk, a Tampa accounting firm. A company spokeswoman said the firm bought it for a client, who declined comment to The Times-Union.

The second is a Colorado-based firm that, according to its Web site, specializes in tax lien and tax certificate purchases. The firm's top executive did not return a phone call seeking comment.

After giving everyone time to read the excerpts from the article, Lauren said, "Remember I told you there were more reasons than you can count as to how someone can lose their property through a tax sale? It happens all the time.

"Look at the date on this article, it is recent. The interest just keeps accumulating no matter who you are. Where else can you find an investment where the interest rate can't go down?"

Allison said, "Lauren, I have to admit that I have been really skeptical about whether or not this could really be used to make someone totally financially independent."

"Even rich," Trish added.

Lauren said, "It does take a while to get your arms around everything. I understand that. That is why I give you so much information on how to verify this for yourself. Let me ask you, if all this is true, and you can see for yourselves that it is true, wouldn't it be terribly irresponsible to *not* take part in it?" Every one nodded in agreement.

"Okay let's move on. Much of the property sold at tax auctions is vacant land. Sometimes there are houses or business structures on the property, but more often it is vacant land. When there is a good building the bidding is usually pretty competitive. But there are still great bargains, as you see in the reprint I just gave you.

"If you really become knowledgeable of land opportunities you will be able to buy great investments for just 1% to 20% of the land's true value.

"Just because a piece of land can't be built on doesn't make it worthless. Because of what you are learning, you have a tremendous advantage over the uneducated investors who just dismiss a piece of property out of hand because you can't build a house on it.

"It all comes down to the location. For example you could; lease the mineral rights, you can lease the land for a highway billboard, you can lease the land for camping or hunting, you can lease the grazing rights for cattle.

"Of course not every parcel will qualify for one of these opportunities, but you are looking for that jewel among the lumps of coal. There are real bargains out there.

"Charlie Daniels was the previous State Land Commissioner of Arkansas. He said that most people were amazed that they would auction really valuable land for such bargain prices. He said that was understandable because most people just don't deal with the issue of delinquent taxes every day. It didn't seem at all unusual to him."

Aaron said, "You know this is all great and you are proving step-by-step that this all works just the way you say, but this is starting to look like a lot of work. I sure don't mind the work; I am just worried about the time it takes."

"That is a legitimate concern," Lauren said. "This is why I am showing you so many ways to take advantage of Tax Defaulted Investment Opportunities. I know you won't do all of them, at least not right away.

"If you are only building your IRA or 401k with Tax Lien Certificates, you will spend very little time. Tax Deeds require more knowledge and research therefore, more time. You will find what fits your needs best and specialize in that area. The area of specialization will probably change over time. Don't forget, I am here to help you, if you want.

"Knowledge is power. You have the power to do these things on your own at your own pace. You can operate this as a home based business, if you set it up correctly."

"I lose sight of that sometimes," Aaron replied.

"I understand. But let's get back to our drawing board. There are a couple of things we haven't talked about when researching an investment.

"For instance you want to learn about IRS liens that a property owner may have filed against him that can cloud the title. This needn't be a problem, if you know what to do. You have already learned that you can get this information from the County Clerk's Office, or the County Recorder in some states.

"I have heard people say that you just shouldn't buy a property that has an IRS lien. First of all IRS liens are filed against individuals and not properties. However the lien usually covers everything the taxpayer owns. So in that sense it is a lien against the property.

"Does this mean you have a major problem? Not necessarily. I know one individual who searches for properties with IRS liens. He understands what to do. The IRS scares most people off which leaves him with very little competition.

"The IRS, by federal statute, has 120 days to redeem this property, if they choose. If they choose to do so, a rare instance, they would have to pay you all the money you have invested plus a 5% penalty.

"Another thing to be aware of is property that is covered by a government insured loan such as FHA and VA loans. The government has one year to redeem those loans. You would not lose your money, they would just pay you off but it can take a while to recoup your money.

"I have never known anyone who has had a problem with these loans. These loans are government *insured*. The government did not lend the money directly. The lending institution is rarely going to allow one of these properties to be foreclosed and wipe them out. They will pay the taxes, expenses and interest to keep that from happening.

"There is one area that can cause a problem that could cost you more than your investment. There can be environmental problems. For example, if the property previously had a gas station on it, the gas tanks could have leaked and it can be horribly expensive to clean it up. It could cost more than the property is worth. This could be why the owners quit paying taxes. They didn't want the property and neither should you.

"Even farm land can be declared marsh land and only good for nesting geese and ducks. Certainly you don't want to take the chance of owning it.

"If a property owner has been sued in civil court and the person, or entity, who brought the suit has won a judgment, there may be a lien filed against the property owner, and everything he or she owns.

"You are scaring me away from investing in Tax Deeds," Eric said. "There just seems to be so many pitfalls it just seems it would be difficult to find a property that isn't a potential land mine."

"You are partially right. There are land mines but there are paths through even the most treacherous minefields. You just have to know where the mines are. I am pointing out the things you should be aware of to get safely through the field.

"I have taught you how to research property. You just need to make a check list of the pitfalls and as you get into your research just scratch each item off your list as you eliminate them.

"For example, if you check with the County Clerk and learn that there are no IRS liens or lawsuits against the owner, just tic that item off your list. Check to see if the property is in an industrial area, or was previously a service station site. You can tick off environmental problems. Once you have run through the research a half dozen times for practice, you can complete your research in about ten minutes.

"Unless I am looking at an exceptional property, I stop the research at the first sign of trouble. This probably causes me to miss some great opportunities, but it also keeps me out of trouble.

"When you are looking at thousands, or tens of thousands, of dollars profit, a few minutes, or even hours, is a small price to pay for a huge payday.

"I am always amazed that people will turn over huge sums of money to someone they have never met, such as a fund manager, without a moment's hesitation then scream like a mashed cat at doing a little work to take charge of their own future.

"Who do you think has your best interest at heart, you or some stranger?"

Eric blushed and said, "I feel like I have just been taken to the woodshed. Lauren, I see your point, I didn't mean to complain, and I apologize."

"No apology necessary. Eric, I was a little harsh with you, but this is your future and you need to be totally engaged in taking care of it. I know you and Allison have three kids and these strategies can secure their future. So I get a little passionate sometimes."

Eric looked at the others and Allison smacked the back of his hand. He knew he would get teased about getting chastised by the teacher.

Lauren smiled at Allison and continued, "You know how I keep saying that things work differently in different states and sometimes even in different counties.

"I have saved, what Kevin will tell you is the best for last. As you all know, because he points it out to everyone, Kevin is from Texas. So let's just see what Kevin has to brag about. Then we really will break for lunch."

"Just ask anyone from Texas, especially Kevin, and they can spend hours telling you how it is just a different kind of place. So you would expect Tax Deeds to be handled differently in Texas than anywhere else. You will learn that they are different.

"Let me just share a few of these differences.

"Most states hold Tax Lien Certificate and Tax Deed sales every year. You have a chance to invest once every twelve months; in Texas you have a chance every month.

"Texas is a deed state; there are no Tax Lien Certificates. You are about to learn about *Restricted Deeds* in Texas. You will see that a Texas Restricted Deed has all the attributes of a Tax Lien Certificate, and more. They are very similar to what you learned about Georgia.

"When you purchase a deed at a Texas auction, you are receiving title to the real estate. However the restriction on the deed gives the property owner six months to redeem the property. If they don't redeem within the six months the deed becomes *absolute* in real estate terms. You don't have to go back to the county and get another deed. It is *absolute* and absolutely yours at the end of six months automatically.

"Texas has 254 counties. Far more than any other state and sales are conducted on the first Tuesday of each month. Not every county has a sale every month because in some of the more sparsely populated counties there aren't that many tax foreclosures. But somewhere in the state there are hundreds of opportunities every month.

"Also, either you or your representative must be present at the auction. If you live outside the state and still want to invest there you can hire a local attorney to attend the auction and bid for you. This can start to get expensive so you will only want to do this if you are bidding on a property with a large profit potential.

"Not only are there 254 counties with a potential sale every month, there are different kinds of sales.

"In Texas the statutes provide for any taxing entity to begin a foreclosure process against any property that is delinquent. For example; any town can foreclose, any school district can foreclose, any utility district, any hospital district can foreclose and offer properties for sale. This creates thousands and thousands of opportunities every month in Texas. It also means you have to be careful in your research.

"You are rewarded handsomely for your investments in tax defaulted Texas properties. First of all you can realize a 300% annualized return on your investment even if the property owner redeems his/her property.

"While 300% annualized return is terrific, you are buying the property with bigger figures in mind. You are buying the property for your own purposes, not looking for an interest rate or penalty. You can get as much as a 300% yield.

"Here is how. You have already learned that Texas tax deeds have a six month redemption period. They carry a 25% *penalty*. So if a deed is redeemed in the first month you earn the full 25% on your money for just one month so this equates to a 300% yield.

"Because there are so many deed sales, you can quickly re-invest those funds to keep earning the 25% penalty. As you have come to expect, there is an exception, and we will talk about that in a moment.

"The sale process in Texas works pretty much the same as it does in other states. When property taxes are delinquent the taxing authority can file a lawsuit to collect the taxes. If they remain unpaid the property will be sold at a public auction to the highest bidder.

"The exception I mentioned applies to what is termed *Homestead Property.* In Texas a property owner can declare his home a homestead, and file for a homestead exemption. Most property carries a six month redemption period. Homestead property has a two year redemption period. Here are the rules effecting a homestead exemption.

Illustration 17

Tax Exemptions, Limitations and Qualification Dates
• **General Residence Homestead:** You may only apply for residence homestead exemptions on one property in a tax year. A homestead exemption may include up to 20 acres of land that you actually use in the residential use

(occupancy) of your home. Arbitrary factors that are unrelated to that use, such as acreage limits, matching legal descriptions, and contiguous parcels, may not be considered in determining if the land qualifies. To qualify for a homestead exemption, you must own and reside in your home on January 1 of the tax year. If you temporarily move away from your home, you still can qualify for an exemption if you don't establish another principal residence and you intend to return in a period of less than two (2) years. Homeowners in military service outside the U.S. or in a facility providing services related to health, infirmity or aging may exceed the two year period

---

"There are lots of counties in Texas so there are lots of rules. I can't give you the rules on every county but I can give you some examples.

"You have to conduct property searches a little differently in Texas. The collection of taxes and filing suits to foreclose on delinquent owners in most states are handled by the county. In Texas all this is handled by a handful of law firms. You may have to call the County Assessor to learn which firm and their contact information.

Matt asked, "How do I know if a property has a homestead exemption?"

Lauren shook her head and smiled, "Again, that 'exception' comes in to play. Here is an example. You can go to http://www.txcountydata.com and get information on several, but by no means all, Texas counties.

"A search result at that site looks like this:

Illustration 18

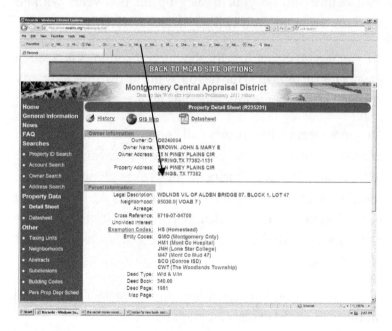

"There are two things I want to point out here: First of all under 'Exemption Code' we see that there is a Homestead Exemption, also you learned previously that there are several taxing entities that can foreclose for unpaid taxes. As you see here there are six different entities; everything from the county, to a hospital district to the Woodlands Township.

"As you have seen in *Illustration 17* Homestead exemptions must be filed, and the people must live on the property on January 1 of the tax year.

"Unless the property you are interested in buying at auction is a tremendous opportunity, you need to think long and hard before you tie your money up for two years without absolute assurance you will get it back before then.

"If you are investing just for the interest earnings it is still a great rate of return. But if you want to own the property you will stay away from properties with an exemption.

"It may seem that nearly all properties will have an exemption and that just isn't the case. Kevin was in the real estate finance business in Texas long ago. He foreclosed on lots of properties. But he told me that not one of them had a homestead exemption. Lots of people don't see any advantage to filing and others just never get around to it.

"After lunch you will learn how to completely get around all the homestead exemption requirements.

"One thing you want to be especially diligent about is recording your deed. The exemption period does not start until you record the deed. So as soon as you receive a deed you need to record it. That starts the six month or two year clock.

"You have seen a couple of challenges but the profit potential, if you do your due diligence, offsets all the challenges. There are challenges to buying tax sale property anywhere. By the time you spend a little time looking at real estate in different counties, you will learn that the research in Texas isn't any more difficult than in other states; it is just different.

"Here is a great positive that you don't find in all other states. The foreclosure and auction in Texas, unlike several other states, extinguishes all other liens except Federal Liens.

"The simplest, and best, title research is done by title companies. You can get a local title company to research property for you for a small fee if you promise them that you will purchase the title policy through them, if you are the successful bidder."

"Are all properties sold at the auction?" Trish wanted to know.

"What a great segue into my next point. No they are not always sold. If the offer is not equal to, or greater than the required opening bid the property is *struck off* to whichever taxing unit that brought the suit.

"Now if you want to spend some time researching properties, this section of the Texas statutes could make you a lot of money.

Section 34.05 (a) and (b)
_____

If a property is sold to a taxing unit, the taxing unit may sell the property by public or private sale---property sold pursuant to Subsections (c) and (d) of this section "may be sold for ANY amount"

"So there can be three kinds of sales—

1. Private counter sales. Here the original minimum bid IS required

2. Private counter sales for LESS THAN the minimum required bid

3. A public auction for LESS THAN the minimum required bid

"To find out about these sales and who will be conducting them you should just call the Tax Assessor's office. They can tell you if they are handling the sale or if a law firm collection agency is handling the sale.

"Be sure to get all your questions answered and the contact information you will need to do your research. Always remember, everything can vary from one county to the next.

"You already know that at the original auction either you, or your representative, must be present. At the struck-off sales, some counties require that you bid by mail. You have to check.

"If this all sounds like a lot of work, think about this. The harder it is to get information, the less your competition. This holds true of everything and every state or county we have discussed, not just in Texas.

Chapter 8

KEVIN DROPS A BOMB

"Success is not created by luck. It is a formula."

- Anonymous

The three couples had placed their lunch order at the Applebee's Restaurant a few blocks from Lauren's office. Trish looked at the others with a puzzled expression, "Wow! I have never had so much information in such a short time. Am I the only one who doesn't know what we should be doing? We have seen so many options."

Eric said, "I don't think we are really expected to know right now. Lauren is just showing us the entire menu and later on when we meet with her we will really start to concentrate on the strategies that best serve our individual needs."

"I'm sure you are right, Eric," Malone said. "I think it will come back to what Kevin has already talked about. It seems a good idea to use the Tax Lien Certificates for the foundation of our plan. This is the only strategy that actually carries a guaranteed rate of return.

"Once we have secured our future with these ultra-safe investments, then we can look at some opportunities to make even more money, even if there is no guarantee, as long as there is minimal risk. My understanding is that we really can't immediately rely on the Tax Lien Certificates for income. Is this the way you see it for us Matt?"

Matt nodded in agreement, and then Aaron asked, "I wonder what surprise Lauren has cooked up for us."

"I don't know. I am surprised and amazed at everything we have been shown so far," Trish said. "I sure never knew that there was any investment anywhere that carried a guaranteed interest rate except bank accounts and some annuities.

"I'll tell you what I did though. I called a few Financial Planners out of the Yellow Pages and asked them if they knew of an investment that carried interest rates of 16% guaranteed by any governmental agency. I called six planners. Two of them actually hung up on me and the others assured me there was no such thing. I didn't tell them, but it is all right there in the statutes of different states, right?"

"Yeah it is," Malone said. "I checked several states and counties. I didn't doubt what Lauren and even Kevin told us, but both of them encouraged us to check it out, so I did"

Everyone had finished lunch and they were all anxious to get back to Lauren's office and get started again.

Lauren smiled at everyone, "I must say you are a bunch of eager beavers. You got back early. That shows the kind of interest that makes my days worthwhile."

"We are anxious to learn about your surprise," Malone said.

"Okay then let's get right to it." As she was talking Kevin came into the room from another office.

"Hi, everyone," he laughed at the surprised looks.

Everyone stood and began to clap. Kevin had handshakes and hugs for everyone.

Lauren said, "Well it is obvious that having Kevin here is a delightful surprise. But Kevin is going to share an even bigger delight for you. The next part of the program involves techniques and strategies that few people have ever heard about. Kevin just happens to be the number one expert in the country, so he is going to share this information with you."

Kevin sat on the front of Lauren's desk facing everyone and crossed his legs. "I am going to tell you a story that I haven't shared with anyone else. I know you all have wondered about how Dagney and I could have such an obvious turn around in our finances."

They all nodded their heads.

"If you haven't thought about it; think of this. First of all we have built a sizeable nest egg in our IRAs and some other tax sheltered vehicles you will learn about a little later. But as you know that money doesn't provide an income right away.

"You have also learned about investing in Tax Deeds. That requires some money and to tell you that Dagney and I had no money when we started would be the understatement of the year.

"Our most pressing need was a quick source of income. So there was no money to buy Tax Deeds, and yet we managed to become very successful investors.

"We started investing in *Opportunity Properties* because we didn't need money to invest. You probably won't see a reference to Opportunity Property anywhere else. This is a term Dagney coined to describe the best money making ideas I have found.

"Next I am going to teach you about Opportunity Properties and how you can do exactly what we did."

"Does that mean we can have a gorgeous estate like you Dagney own?" Trish laughed.

"Well as a matter-of-fact the twenty acre parcel right next to us on the west side is available. We would love to have you as neighbors.

"But on with the story. I was in the finance and insurance business years ago in Lubbock, Texas; long before we ever moved here.

"I was a pretty fair country insurance peddler, so the company promoted me to an Area Manager and transferred us to Albuquerque, New Mexico. Neither Dagney nor I knew much about Albuquerque even though I grew up in Tucumcari, New Mexico, but I was thrilled with the opportunity.

"We dropped our kids off with my parents in Amarillo, Texas and started driving west on I-40 for Albuquerque.

"As we got into New Mexico we started seeing an occasional sign offering land for sale for $15 down and $15 per month. A little farther down the road the signs started being more specific. The land was just outside Moriarty, New Mexico, just over the Sandia Mountains from Albuquerque.

"Just before we got to Moriarty there was a huge billboard that welcomed everyone to **Sweetwater Hills** and these great real estate bargains.

"The land was just prairie and was as flat as a pancake. There wasn't a hill or a tree in sight, just flat land."

Kevin clicked the projector:

Illustration 19

"This is what it looked like. We didn't stop to look at the land that day but I made an offhand remark to Dagney that proved to be very prophetical. I said, 'What if we were moving out here to sell that land?'"

"I don't know how many of you have read, *The Secret,* or have seen the movie. The book and movie are all about the fact that we attract what we think about.

"Well for some reason that thought kind of got caught in my mind. I have always loved sales and enjoy figuring out how to sell different things. I thought about how I would go about selling that land in one or two acre parcels. I have to admit I never came up with an idea, except for those signs along the highway.

"Just over those mountains you see in the distance is Albuquerque. In a few minutes we were driving through those mountains and I didn't think about selling that land again for a year.

"I won't bore you with the details, but in one year I had left the insurance company and was Sales Manager for the company that owned Sweetwater Hills along with a few other developments.

"Obviously, I had figured out how to sell land.

"A few months after developing a tremendous sales team a very fortunate thing happened to me.

"It was the spring of 1971 when Frank Dehoney called me into his office. Frank was the Director of Sales for the land company and I was the number two man as Sales Manager.

"Frank asked me, 'Kevin, how would you like to make a lot of money? Make as much as you want and make it whenever you want?'"

"I thought that was a really strange question. After all I had taken a sales organization that consisted of three people that was going nowhere, built a new sales team and sold more land in the second thirty days I was there than the entire company had sold the previous year.

"I had built the most successful sales organization in Albuquerque, New Mexico. We were so successful that a salesman could only park in front of the office if they were driving a Cadillac. My new one was always parked right in the middle.

"We had almost as many Cadillacs parked at the office, when everyone was together for a sales meeting, as the local Cadillac dealer, Galles Cadillac, often had on his lot.

"I am already making a lot of money; I answered with all the arrogance and foolishness that only a young, suddenly successful, person is capable.

"I know you are, but I am going to share a secret with you that probably less than one hundred people know about." Frank told me.

"Frank then spelled out the program that we now call Opportunity Properties and I am now going to share with you.

"That was the most valuable conversation of my life. The conversation we are having right now will be worth literally millions of dollars to you, if you learn from it and use it.

"At the time Frank shared this information with me it was difficult to use. There was no internet so anything you wanted to know about a property had to be found at local county offices. If you were interested in property from another state you had to go there and research it.

"I know Lauren has already shown you how to research a property. You have seen examples from different states, all while you are sitting here in her office. You could be home on your couch. The Internet has made this strategy easy and at almost zero cost.

"So years later, when Dagney and I needed to really start making money, this is what we turned to and it has made all the difference in the world."

"Is this finally *The Secret Synergy Group System?*" Allison could hardly contain her enthusiasm.

"We will get to that later, but what I want you to know is that the secrets Frank told me, and I am going to share with you now, will teach you *exactly* how to buy $10,000 to $50,000 chunks of real estate for just $25 to $100, sell quickly for many thousands of dollars, then do it over and over as often as you like.

"I was working on a different project than Sweetwater Hills, but that project had a special allure for the tourists who couldn't resist the billboards along I-40. They just couldn't resist the opportunity to own some acreage in the West.

"Many of them bought the land with the intention of building their retirement home there. Some bought just for the investment opportunity.

"I talked to a lot of these owners who came back to visit their Western Ranch, as they often referred to it to their friends back east and up north. They told me of the great pleasure they got from telling their co-workers that they were going to visit their New Mexico ranch during their vacation.

"They told the stories to their fellow workers with a great sense of pride. They told the stories while they were, in many cases, working at a daily grind in a lousy job.

"Many of them did come out during their vacations. They sometimes camped on their land. Some of them did build their retirement home there. Many of them never actually did anything with the land. They eventually paid it off, and in a lot of cases the land was passed on to their children.

"Typically, the children don't share the dreams of their parents so they have no real use for the land. They just have to pay taxes each year and often have grown weary of that. Here is a typical example. This is from an EBay listing.

Illustration 19

(Readable text in Appendix)

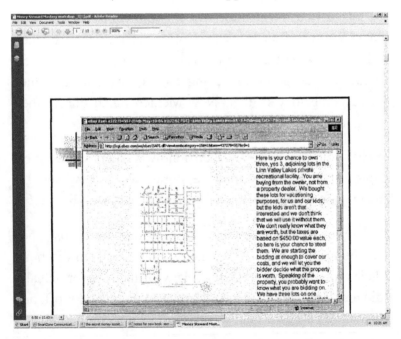

"These folks are typical. They say they bought the land for themselves and their kids and the kids just aren't interested.

So if this land had been passed on to their children, the children would certainly be "Don't Wanters."

"Sometimes heirs list the property with a local Realtor, but the results are usually not very good. The children often have an unrealistic view of the value of the land in the beginning.

"With the land listed at a top dollar, usually unrealistic, price and competing with a lot of other real estate, real estate agents put little effort into selling it. After all why make a $500 or $600 commission on a piece of land when they can make thousands on the sale of a home?

"I can see some of you starting to wonder what this story has to do with you and Opportunity Properties. I tell you the story just to show you how a property becomes an Opportunity Property.

"Any experienced real estate investor will tell you that you make money when you buy real estate. So how do you find these great buys? You look for what the real estate agents call, "Don't Wanters."

"The scenario I have shown you is on just one property in one state. There are literally thousands of subdivisions like the one I described all over the United States.

"The company I worked for had six such subdivisions at the time with thousands of owners scattered throughout the United States.

"Major corporations have been involved in the land business. McCulloch Corporation, famous for chain saws, had many thousands of acres for sale. They had teams of salesmen who traveled all over the country selling these properties at dinner parties. Many of these buyers still have never even seen the property. Whatever reasons they had for buying the property, their circumstances have changed.

"The most famous of McCulloch's developments is Lake Havasu City in Arizona. It is now the site of the famous London Bridge. A very prosperous city has sprung up, literally in the desert.

"Even though there are many homes there, there are even more vacant lots that people bought and never used. Most of these are excellent prospects for the program I am sharing with you.

"There are great developments in almost every state, especially in places like Arizona, Florida, New Mexico, Texas and Arkansas.

"The list could go on and on, but I think you are getting the picture that out of the literally thousands of people who own recreational or retirement property, there are untold thousands who are now serious "Don't Wanters."

"Since there are thousands of owners out there who don't have any more use for these properties, their property can often be bought for very little money, sometimes for nothing.

"Lauren told you, when we met at my house, that one of these people recently wanted to just give me a three unit apartment house. This happens more often than you can imagine.

"The Opportunity Property program boils down to three simple steps.

    1. Find these "Don't Wanters"

2. Show them how they can have money in their pocket, even if they sell their property at a loss

3. Put the property under contract and either buy it or resell it before the closing date of the contract

Matt shook his head, "Come on Kevin it can't possibly be that simple. How do we find these people? What kind of magic is used to put money in their pocket, even if they sell at a loss, and finally how can we sell this real estate when they haven't been able to sell it?"

"Matt I am so happy to see that you are forever the skeptic. Please stay that way. Surely you know me well enough to know that I am not going to tell you a fairy tale. So stay skeptical, pay close attention and don't try to make this complicated.

"I am going to start with the way for these folks to put money in their pocket even if they sell for less than what the property is worth, or what they paid for it.

"Look at this." Kevin clicked the projector to.....

Illustration 20

Topic 409 - Capital Gains and Losses

Capital gains and losses are classified as long-term or short-term. If you hold the asset for more than one year before you dispose of it, your capital gain or loss is long-term. If you hold it one year or less, your capital gain or loss is short-term.

If you have a taxable capital gain, you may be required to make estimated tax payments. Refer to Publication 505, *Tax Withholding and Estimated Tax*, for additional information.

If your capital losses exceed your capital gains, the amount of the excess loss that can be claimed is the lesser of $3,000, ($1,500 if you are married filing separately) or your total net loss as shown on line 16 of the Form 1040 Schedule D, *Capital Gains and Loses*. If your net capital loss is more than this limit, you can carry the loss forward to later years. Use the Capital Loss Carryover Worksheet in Publication 550, to figure the amount carried forward.

Kevin continued, "You need to pay close attention here. The TOPIC 409 you see on your screen is from a page directly from the IRS website www.irs.gov . This tells you that a married couple can deduct up to $3,000 in capital loss in one year. It also says that if the loss is greater than $3,000 they can carry the loss forward to another year. It need not be the next year.

"I will show you how to use this page shortly. What you see on the screen is only the pertinent part of this page from the website. We use it, but you have to be careful. You never tell anyone that they can take a tax deduction. You merely send them a copy of this page and tell them that they may be eligible for the deduction, but they will need to check it with their own CPA."

Malone said, "This looks perfectly clear to me. Why can't we just tell they can take the deduction?"

"This puts you in the position of giving tax advice. If you are not a registered tax advisor you can land in deep trouble. But don't let this frighten you. Just do as I suggested and you are fine.

"So let's see what this means. This deduction reduces their taxable income by $3,000, if the capital loss is that much. So they do not have to pay taxes on $3,000 of their income. A tax deduction usually means cash saving of around one-third of their deduction. In this example they can keep $1,000 that will not have to go to the government. So they have an extra $1,000 in their pocket.

"Let's just take it a step further. Assume that the real estate has a value of $9,000 and they are selling it to you for a token payment of $25." All they eyebrows went up and Kevin laughed, "I know you all want to know how we make that happen. Just stay with me.

"The owners of the real estate have a loss of $9,000 but they can only deduct $3,000 in any one year. So they take the deduction this year. Next year, let's say they have lots of other deductions. They are eligible to take another $3,000 deduction from the real estate, but if they don't need the deduction they can carry it forward to a year when it will be meaningful.

"So even though they are selling you the real estate for just a token, they still put money in their pocket."

"I understand that, but how many are willing to sell at a loss even with the tax break?" Trish wanted to know.

"Oh, very few. Up until recently only one or two percent would sell for just a token. But what if it is only one fourth of one percent, would you mail four hundred letters to get a property for under one hundred dollars?"

Everyone got the picture so Kevin continued, "With the economy in its' present shape there are more and more. More people than ever before are unable or just unwilling to keep paying taxes on something they can't use.

"So that percentage is up considerably and I have a couple of new techniques that Dagney and I have been using with great success. These techniques enable us to get a much better response rate than the one or two percent we got for years. Then we sell the property without ever owning it. But we are getting ahead of ourselves.

"The deduction you have learned about was made possible by the Tax Reform Act of 1986. Prior to this act the maximum deduction was just fifty percent of capital losses. After 1986 thousands and thousands of people have studied the act, but never used it this way.

"I don't know who first came up with this idea, but a small group of insiders have been using the act to their advantage ever since.

"Now to get into the meat of this, here is how it works. It has been working since 1987, and it still works just as well, or better, today.

"The insiders, me included, use these principles all the time. We get a list of people who live in a state other than where the real estate I have been describing is located.

"In other words, if we are getting a list of property owners that own the New Mexico properties I told you about, we only want the ones that do not live in New Mexico.

"We write them a letter similar to these." Kevin said as he handed them copies of three different letters. *(Author's note: You can get a free copy of the letters by just emailing jimyocom@comcast.net and asking that they be sent to you. There is no obligation and we do not share your name or email address with anyone, under any circumstances.)*

"The easiest, and best, way to start is to target the out of state property owners who are not keeping the taxes current on their property.

"Some of these owners will be the "Don't Wanters" we talked about. We send one of the letters you have, or a variation of one of them. This tells them that we found their name during our research on investments in *"Paradise Acres"* development and see that they have not paid their property taxes.

"We tell them that if their plans have changed and they have less interest in the property than when they first acquired it, we may have a solution for them.

"We include a copy of the *Topic 409* from the IRS website. We explain that by selling the property for a token payment they could be able to take a tax deduction for the difference between the token payment and the value of the property.

"We go to great lengths to make sure we can never be accused of giving tax or legal advice.

"Now to get back to your question Trish, only one or two percent of these folks are anxious to accept our offer.

"That's okay. This rejection is pretty easy to handle. Consider this. If we send out one hundred letters and get one or two people to accept our offer, and we make a profit of $3,000 to $10,000, how bad is that? Where else can we fail ninety-nine times out of a hundred and still be a resounding success?

"I have kept some of the emails I have found over the years concerning the success some people have had. Here are some examples."

Kevin clicked the next slide.

Illustration 21

ALL LETTERS ARE ON FILE

One person tells of eight parcels that was purchased for between $10 and $100 each. They listed them for $12,000 to $49,000 each and cleared a profit of over $150,000

Another one tells of buying three unwanted properties for $1,500 and a Realtor listed them for what he thinks they are worth: $35,000 EACH – similar properties are selling at auction for $20,000 each.

One very fortunate person tells of buying 2 lots for $25 each with an appraisal of $5,000 each. Got 5 lots free and clear from a builder for $25 each which are appraised for a total of $60,000. Also bought a lot with a mobile home for $100 with a $21,800 appraisal. All this from mailing 200 letters. **(I have never seen anyone else with these results.)**

Still another one tells of buying 41 properties in 9 months – all for $10 to $25 each.

Others tell these stories....

- *"Sold property for $10,300, paid $50 for it."*

- *Paid $50, took one year to sell it for $22,500."*

- *"--bought 200 properties all with Fair Market Value of at least $10,000 the first year and have already sold over 1/2 of them. Will send 300 letters per week and will get 4.5 deeds per week."*

- *From Colorado - "From March to December bought 41 properties for $10 to $25."*

- *"Buys properties in CA, OR, WA, MA for $100 or less, bought 73 in 11 months."*

- *"--paid $20 assessed at $59,000."*

"Good grief, is this for real?" Aaron wanted to know.

"Well the people who wrote these letters had nothing to gain, so I take them at their word, especially knowing my own experience. Bear in mind these excerpts from letters are from people who were doing what almost everyone does. They get these results from offering token payments and getting a one or two percent response.

"I am going to share a method that gets as much as a five and ten percent response. Though, I have actually gotten a twenty percent response. But first let's look at some different sources of leads.

"There are lots of ways to get lists of people you can mail to. An easy place is a list of Tax Lien Certificates that are coming up for sale. You know, without having to do any research, that they are delinquent on their taxes. There is a great website www.TaxSaleLists.com that gives you all the information you want. They tell you weekly of upcoming sales. You can get the upcoming lists and also lists from years past. This is all I use.

"We have already discussed the lists you can subscribe to from Arkansas. Arkansas has a lot of resort areas, and here is a list just handed to you. All you have to do is research the county to get the mailing address of the owners of each of these properties."

Allison said, "You talk mostly about properties in resort areas. Does that mean that other locations aren't worth mailing?"

"Allison, thank you for bring that up. I talk about resort properties because that is where most of the opportunities lie. Let's just look lots inside any town or city. Take the neighborhood where you live. How many vacant lots are there in your neighborhood?"

"Actually, I can't think of any."

"Precisely! Now there are exceptions to everything we talk about, but generally speaking most people buy city lots because they are ready, or near ready, to build a home on it.

"Vacation property is usually bought with a lot more emotion. For example they are on vacation in the Ozarks and fall in love with the country. They play a round of golf in a subdivision and learn that there are numerous lots available. They find that they can take advantage of the golf course or any other facilities as property owners.

"They start talking about how great it would be to retire there, or just have a vacation cottage. Before you know it they have bought their piece of paradise.

"But, as we have seen, as years go by those dreams change and this presents us with lots of opportunities.

"When the economy changes or they lose their jobs, they start looking for ways to pare down their expenses. About this time they get a bill for the taxes on the lot. Usually the taxes are very low, but it is just another expense. Or maybe they just come to the realization that they will never be able to build their dream home of the lot. Either way, they are becoming "Don't Wanters."

"I just look for Tax Lien Certificates that are approaching the end of the redemption period. These property owners are in real danger of losing their property. Many of them would much rather get some money via income tax reduction than to lose the property outright, even though they may not really want it any longer.

I can get all this information from www.TaxSaleLists.com.

"If they are foreclosed they can't take a tax deduction. A little money is better than none at all, and they don't want the foreclosure on their record.

"When you send out the letters, you are going to get a lot of them back marked "Undeliverable" for various reasons. If they came back to you that means that the tax notices were not delivered either, because you are mailing to the same address as the county.

"If you bought the Tax Lien Certificate, do you think there is a greater chance that these properties just may not be redeemed and your odds of acquiring the properties if you own a Tax Lien Certificate are increased?

It is worthwhile to see if you can locate these people and let them know they are about to lose their property. Most of the time they have just abandoned the property and are happy to get even a token and escape foreclosure.

"There is a lot to be gained by this letter writing technique. Of course it requires some work. I can't tell you how many nights Dagney and I have stayed up late addressing envelopes, but it has paid off.

"We don't do that anymore. We use a service at www.click2mail.com that prints and mails them for us.

"What if you were doing this as your home based business? Now you have to check this out with your CPA, but if done correctly it can qualify as a legitimate home based business.

The tax deductions from having a home based business will more than pay your expenses in printing and mailing. I am going to spend some time with you a little later to acquaint you with the advantages of a home based business. For now, let's just say that you MUST have a home based business.

"This doesn't even take into consideration the amount of money you are going to make when you resell the properties.

"Your imagination is the only limitation placed on this letter writing technique. Using the same techniques used to acquire lists, there are some people who prefer to call these property owners rather than write the letters.

"I am sure this is a great technique. It doesn't appeal to me. First of all I don't have time to spend hours on the phone. You will spend some time on the phone with people who receive your letter and call you. Make it easy for them. In your letters include your phone number, your cell phone number, your FAX number, your email address and any other way they can get in touch with you. These are dollars calling and you don't want to miss the call.

"Okay, let's take a fifteen minute break. I need some coffee."

Chapter 9

KEVIN PUTS THE PROGRAM ON STEROIDS

How I made my fortune?

It was really quite simple. I bought an apple for five cents, spent the evening polishing it, and sold it the next day for ten cents. With this I bought two apples, spent the evening polishing them, and sold them for twenty cents. And so it went until I had amassed $1.60. It was then that my wife's father died and left us a million dollars

--Anonymous Capitalist

"I hope everyone got a chance to stretch your legs." Kevin said.

Aaron said, "Okay Kevin, come clean. We all want to know about this *Secret Synergy Group System.* Are you going to tell us now?"

Kevin laughed. It was obvious he was enjoying their curiosity. "In due course it will be revealed. There will be a pillar of smoke, then out will jump the Genie and all will be revealed."

"I will take that as a 'NO."

"It is not a 'NO, it is just a 'Not Now.' But think about this. Do you know the dictionary definition of the word *secret?*"

"Well not exactly what the dictionary says." Aaron answered.

Kevin said, "The *OXFORD ENGLISH DICTIONARY* says, *"A mystery. Something no one properly understands; a method (not known to everyone) for attaining something;"*

"So do you feel that what you are learning is something that is not known to everyone? Do you feel like it is a mystery?"

"It certainly wasn't known by any of us, and a lot of it is still a mystery." Aaron answered.

"Okay, just stay with me. Once we get all the pieces of the puzzle on the table and all of them turned face up, I'll assemble the pieces and you'll see a beautiful picture.

"Before the break I mentioned the website www.TaxSaleLists.com a couple of times. I am not going to point out everything on the site; you can check it out for yourselves. It is very user friendly. I do want you to know what I use.

"You will need to join the site. You can join and get a lot of information for no charge. Later you will probably pay for a membership. I think it is still around $300 for a full year and I can get an unlimited number of lists.

"After you join, you can pick a state and click that state on the map. You will find information about sales going back five years. I like Arizona and I like to get lists that are three years old. Can anyone guess why?"

"Probably because Arizona has a three year redemption period." Allison said.

"You have been paying attention and you are exactly right. I want to be able to use time as a motivator for the owners to make a decision.

"So now I have my list. When you look at the spreadsheet in Xcel form you will find a ton of information and maybe thousands of properties. So we have to start sorting the list down to the point where it looks like the one on the screen.

"The first thing I want to do is eliminate every property owner address in Arizona. As you know, I am looking for owners of Arizona real estate that live somewhere other than Arizona.

"My next sort is by price. I like land so in the past I looked for real estate values between $5,000 and $50,000. With one of the techniques I am going to show you, I want to make offers on everything. But even with this broad search most of the parcels left will be land with nothing built on it. If there was a house on the land the taxes probably would be paid off before now.

"Now, here is where I do things a little different than the way most people do. A lot of people will get their list of out of state property owners and research every property.

"I am not interested in knowing everything, or even anything, about a property that I have no possibility of making an offer. I go ahead and send letters to all of them, then when I have a positive conversation, either by phone or email, I make an offer and if it is accepted then I research the property thoroughly.

"Do I sometimes learn something bad about a deal after my offer has already been accepted? Sure I do. But I always write my offers with a way to get out of a bad situation. For example, here is a phrase I put in every offer; whether it is a purchase offer or an option." As he said this, Kevin passed a sheet of paper to each person with the phrase printed on the sheet.

This agreement is subject to approval of condition of title and property condition. Should Buyer *(Optionee)* determine that property is not suitable for acquisition due to title problems, unusual property conditions or any other reason Buyer *(Optionee)* will not record the deed and will destroy all papers including the deed, or return them to Seller, and agreement will be cancelled. Seller shall retain the purchase *(Option)* price paid by Buyer *(Optionee)* as full consideration of cancellation of this agreement. Regardless of whether Buyer *(Optionee)* elects to record deed or cancel this agreement, Seller understands and agrees that Buyer *(Optionee)* has not promised to pay any taxes, mortgages or liens against this property. Buyer may elect not to do so until a suitable third party purchaser is found for the property. Both parties agree that Buyer is purchasing the property in as-is condition and Seller makes no warranty as to property or title condition.

"Some people refer to this as a 'Weasel Clause' because you can weasel out of the deal. I don't like that terminology, but it is an apt description. This phrase would be modified if you are negotiating on an expensive property where a title policy would be involved. Right now we are just talking about small pieces of land; a home site, or maybe even a few acres.

"My preferred way to handle these purchases is with a Quit Claim Deed. This is the simplest way to deed property and is just as legitimate and accepted as any other form of deed.

"Some people like to insist on a Warranty Deed, and I do too if the property is a house or commercial building."

Eric said, "I have heard that Quit Claim Deeds are not acceptable to title companies or sophisticated investors. Is this true?"

"I have never heard of a title company that would not accept a QCD, as it is called in real estate circles. Actually they have no choice, if the QCD is recorded it legitimately transfers ownership."

"What is the difference," Eric wanted to know.

Kevin said, "As far as legally conveying title, there is none. The difference has to do with the seller. A seller gives a QCD that says that whatever interest they have in a specific property they convey it to the buyer. The seller isn't making any claims or warranties about the condition of the property or the title.

"Here is where I think some people get confused. I can legally give you a QCD on the Empire State Building. All the deed is saying is that whatever interest I have in the building, I am deeding to you. Now I don't have any interest in the building so I have given you nothing. In the deed I don't claim to have any ownership or interest in the building. So because, in this example, the deed is worthless some people are confused in thinking that a QCD is perhaps worthless.

"If I give you a Warranty Deed on a certain property, I am warranting, or guaranteeing, whatever is spelled out in the

Warranty Deed. This usually is the status of the title. I can warrant that there are no liens, Deeds of Trust etc. that could cloud the title. If later it is found that this is not the case you can sue me for damages.

"With many of the people who are selling or giving us the land, their assets are not sufficient to cover damages if we should win a lawsuit. So their warranty is worthless and the Warranty Deed doesn't guarantee anything that a QCD does not.

"You need to remember this, not just for your own good, but you may have to explain it to someone who is buying from you.

"If you are dealing with a property that has a substantial profit potential you can spend just a little money, usually around $150, with a title company and add a good selling point to your property.

"You can ask a title company for a *Title Search*, not a *Title Policy*. The title company will do basically the same research for either instrument. The difference is that the Title Search just lists their findings while a title policy insures the condition of the title that is specified by the Title Company."

"You have already learned to research a piece of real estate. I use what I have learned in the research, which is the same research done by a title company, and pass that information along to a potential buyer. I show screenshots from the County Clerk, or County Recorder, that shows everything pertaining to the particular property.

"If this shows that there are no outstanding liens other than taxes, I am satisfied, and I find this satisfies most potential buyers. I also show a screen shot from the Assessor's office that shows any delinquent taxes."

"Okay, at the risk of sounding really dumb, you talk about the offer to buy the real estate and you talk about getting an option. I don't even know what an offer like you are talking about looks like." Allison was truly puzzled.

"Thank you for that, Allison," Kevin said. I get excited and sometimes get ahead of myself. Actually I am surprised that Lauren hasn't already gotten on my case."

"You are doing fine. But this is probably just the right place to explain to all of them a little more detail about the different kinds of offers and what they look like." Lauren said.

"Thanks," Kevin said. "There are lots of ways to make offers. As you pointed out, Allison, we make offers to purchase the real estate and we make offers to get an option to purchase the real estate.

"The Option to Purchase Real Estate is just what it sounds like. We are seeking the right to purchase a parcel of real estate by some date in the future, at a price we agree on with the seller. The option gives us the right to purchase, but we are not obligated to purchase it."

Allison was still puzzled, "Okay, I think I understand what you said, but how do we know when we want to purchase, and when do we want an option. It seems they do pretty much the same thing."

"They do actually do the same thing; we are seeking to acquire a particular parcel of real estate. The difference is whether we are actually obligated or not.

"If we make an offer to purchase the real estate and the owner accepts the offer, we are obligated to go ahead with the purchase. While there is an accepted offer on the real estate, the owner cannot accept an offer from anyone else, so his property is tied up awaiting us to close on it. If we don't close, he can sue us for damages, and in most cases he will collect, so we have to be careful with offers, because they carry legal consequences.

"The owner also cannot sell his property to anyone else while there is an open and accepted option on it. However, to make it good for both the owner and us, I often use what is called a 'Flex Option.' I'll explain that in just a moment.

"Remember I mentioned a 'weasel clause' before? This just gives us a way out of the contract. Not all owners will accept an offer with a 'weasel clause.' But almost all offers have some sort of clause in it, so it isn't something new. I'll show you how we make both the Purchase Offer and the Option acceptable in most cases.

"Bear in mind, we are talking about Opportunity Properties. If you are buying a house for yourself, it will be handled differently, and the Realtor will do all this for you. We rarely use a Realtor because we don't want to be out the expense of the commission.

"To decide which offer to make, let's look at what we are trying to accomplish. We rarely want to buy any real estate. We just want to make money on it. If we buy it, we need to already have someone else lined up to buy it from us. We want to just turn the real estate, make money and go on to the next transaction.

"There are several ways to do this. The ideal way is to get a contract, or option, find a buyer before closing date and just assign our contract to this new buyer. To allow us to do this, there must be an 'Assignment Clause' in either offer that allows us to do this.

"For example we get a contract to purchase or an option to buy for $40,000. We find a buyer who is willing to pay $50,000. We assign the contract to him for a fee of $10,000. He pays us the $10,000; he exercises the option, or closes on the contract with the seller and pays the seller $40,000."

"Isn't this new buyer going to be reluctant to pay us $10,000 when he knows we have it under contract for $40,000? Why wouldn't he just go directly to the owner and make the deal with him?" Matt wanted to know.

"Remember I told you that the owner can't sell to anyone else while we have the property under contract? I can already anticipate your next question. Why wouldn't he just wait until our offer expires and then deal directly with the owner?"

"Exactly. Why wouldn't he?" Matt asked.

"There is nothing to stop him, and it does happen sometimes. But if this new buyer is convinced he is getting what he wants and that $50,000 is a fair price it usually doesn't matter. Besides, with Opportunity Properties, we are usually buying at such a bargain price that we have a lot of wiggle room if we have to negotiate.

"However, there is a solution. We can go ahead and close on the property in our name then resell to the new buyer at whatever price we negotiate."

"Oh sure, I'll just buy dozens of properties out of my ready cash, then hope for a buyer." Aaron was obviously displeased with this solution.

"What if I told you that you could buy a multi-million dollar property tomorrow, finance it 100%, not make a down payment and never even have your credit checked? Would that relieve some of your tension?"

"Come on Kevin, we know that isn't possible." Aaron was still frowning.

"Well, as far as you know at this moment, that isn't possible, but you are going to have full knowledge of exactly how to do this before the day is over. I am going to show you how and where to get the money, and I am going to show you another way that works without your money, and is also done all the time."

"Okay, I'll bite, what is this magic formula?"

"It is a formula, but there is nothing magical about it. The second method I mentioned is called a double closing. Title companies know how to handle this and do it regularly. This will not work this way if you are dealing with more expensive properties that require outside financing, if that financing is going to go through Fannie Mae or Freddie Mac. Now I am not going into those types of transactions. We are just talking about Opportunity Properties.

"It works like this. The Title Company handles both transactions; the one where you buy the property and the second one where you sell the property to a new buyer. This is called an A to B and B to C transaction. **A** is the

Opportunity Property owner. He sells to **B**, which is you. You sell to **C**, which is the end buyer.

"All the paperwork is completed in advance, and both closings take place the same day. You do not bring any money to the closing table to pay off your seller. But you are going to sell the property to the new buyer the same day.

"The Title Company takes the money that was obtained from the new buyer and it goes into their trust account; $50,000 to continue with our example.

"$40,000 goes to your seller of the Opportunity Property. There is $10,000 left over and that goes to you. The new buyer doesn't know, and doesn't need to know what you paid for the property.

"This was always easy until the recent government sponsored crash of the real estate market. Now because of some issues with Fannie and Freddie some Title Companies just don't handle these closings any more. But it isn't hard to find the name of a title company that will.

"The other way that I mentioned works a little differently. You are actually borrowing the $40,000, plus enough to pay all expenses, and the lending company wire transfers funds directly into the title company trust account. Then it works the same way. $40,000 from the wire transfer goes to the Opportunity Property Owner. The title company takes the $50,000 certified funds from the new buyer and uses $40,000 to pay off your loan and then sends you the $10,000.

"This is a little over simplified because the title company also has to pay expenses out of these funds also. Your check will not be quite $10,000 because you will have to pay for the funds you borrowed for one day and any other expenses, so these will be deducted from your $10,000."

"And you are going to line us up with someone who will make these loans to close these deals. Do I understand this right?" now Matt is asking.

"Oh I'll show you where these lenders are and you can take your pick. This is just routine business for them. They could care less about your assets, your credit score, or your ability to repay. You see it all comes from the funds of the new buyer. We will get into this a little deeper in a few minutes.

Eric said, "Kevin, this gets more exciting by the minute. I hope you aren't going to drop a bombshell on us and shatter that enthusiasm."

"Oh, there will be no bombshell. In fact I am just laying the groundwork. You are going to need some Dramamine to stop your head from spinning.

"Besides, I know how you feel. I was the same way before I met Lauren. Dagney and I knew about Tax Lien Certificates, Tax Deeds, Struck Off Properties, Opportunity Properties and most of what we have been talking about. But it took Lauren's knowledge to show us how to actually use all these strategies to our greatest benefit. We were just like you; we had never heard of this kind of financing either, and we were even more skeptical than you guys."

Lauren was just sitting quietly behind her desk. Eric turned to her and said, "Wow you must be a really great teacher, if you are the one that taught Kevin and Dagney. We are listening to Kevin and he is so knowledgeable it seems that he is the teacher. I am glad he gives you credit where it is due."

"He is overly generous. But for those that decide to go all the way with these strategies, you will be able to teach others just as Kevin is teaching you."

"I think I am starting to figure out this *Secret Synergy Group System.* We learn then help teach others, is that it?" Trish asked.

"Careful about dipping your toe in that water," Kevin laughed. "You don't want to get immersed before you are ready. But we are circling the field now. We will be landing pretty soon, then you see the puff of smoke and all is revealed.

"Seriously, let's just take a few more minutes and talk about our offer and what goes into it.

"An offer needs to be written and actually you can write it on the back of an envelope. If both parties agree to what is written and sign it, it is as legal as if it had been written on the finest form prepared by the greatest lawyer in the land.

"However, sometimes the parties disagree on what is written and they wind up in court trying to defend or challenge the envelope. That is why we make offers on forms that has language that has already stood up in court.

"For most Opportunity Property transactions one of these forms is all that is needed. But if it is a large transaction, and you have written some terms or exclusions into the contract, you should probably get a lawyer to handle it. A lawyer will charge far less to prepare a contract than he will to defend it in court.

"So where do we get these contracts, if we don't use a lawyer?" Malone wanted to know.

You will find most of the contracts you will need at, http://reitips.com/free-forms-download/ at no cost."

Kevin clicked on *Illustration 22* and said, "Here is an Option Agreement directly from the REI website. I want to call your attention to number 4 under Terms and Conditions, this is what makes this work so well. This relieves all the pressure on the property owner. He has everything to gain, and nothing to lose.

"If he gets a better offer while you are looking for a buyer, he can cancel the option with you and sell it himself. This is the weakest offer we can make, but also the easiest to sell to the owner. It does leave us open to having the agreement pulled from us just as we are in serious negotiations with a buyer. But if the owner has been actively trying to sell the property, with no success, it is unlikely that he will suddenly find a buyer. Most of the time you will find that he isn't making any effort to sell at all.

Illustration 22

Option to Purchase Real Estate Agreement

I. Contract Date: _____

II. This Option Agreement is made between the following parties:

---

    1.   _____,
       hereinafter referred to as "Optionor" and

2. _____,

hereinafter referred to as "Optionee".

III. Real Property: The Optionor agrees to grant an option to purchase to the Optionee, the land and improvements known as:_____

_____

IV. Offer: Optionee has the option to purchase this property for the price of $_____.

V. Period: 14 days, beginning on the contract date and ending on _____.

VI. Terms and Conditions:

1. Optionor understands that Optionee intends to find an End-Buyer (i.e. new buyer) and assign this Option Agreement to End-Buyer for a fee (to be paid by End-Buyer).

2. Optionor understands that Optionee is acting as a principle in the transaction and is not working as a real estate broker representing anyone other than himself in this transaction.

3. Upon Optionee exercising of this option, both parties agree to move forward with the necessary standard purchase and sales agreement.

4. Optionor may cancel this agreement at any time at any time prior to exercise should he find his own Optionee or tenant or decide not to sell. This cancellation must be done in writing.

5. Optionor grants Optionee access to the above property for showing to prospective buyers, contractors, or appraisers, along with the right to put signage in the yard advertising the property for sale.

6. If Optionee does not acquire an End-Buyer within 14 days of acceptance of this Option Agreement, this agreement becomes null and void.

7. All parties agree that property is being sold in present "as is" condition.

8. Optionor must ensure that proper insurance is maintained on the property.

9. Optionor grants this option for the consideration of ten dollars ($10.00) and other valuable consideration.

10. Time is of the essence in this agreement.

VII. Additional   **Terms:**

_____

_____

_____

_____

Optionee: _____

_____ **Date:** _____

Phone/Email/Fax:

_____

_____

Optionor:

_____

_ **Date:** _____

Phone/Email/Fax: _____

"You will find another option agreement on the website that actually ties up the property. I suggest that you attempt to get this option every time. If that is not possible, this is your 'Plan B.' If that is not possible, this is your 'Plan B.' This agreement is known as a 'Flex Option."

Malone raised her hand and asked, "Don't we need a real estate license to sell property that we don't own?"

"I was wondering when someone was going to question this. Good catch, Malone. The answer is yes we need a license to sell real estate if we have no ownership or interest. The option, or the offer to purchase, gives us what is known in legal terminology as an 'Equitable Interest' in the property. You don't need a license to sell your own home, or any other property in which you have an Equitable Interest.

"If you are nervous about a seller trying to go around you, the website I gave you has an Equitable Interest form and an Affidavit of Equitable Interest form. You can have the seller sign these and you can record the Affidavit. This prevents the seller from encumbering the property or selling it during the term of the agreement.

"You always want to make sure you have the phrase shown as number 1 in all your offers, whether an option or offer to purchase."

"These things come into play when we get into more expensive property. In the beginning I recommend that you stay with the less expensive land deals that are owned by serious 'Don't Wanters.'

"Now let's learn how to put this all together in a system. The first step is to decide on which state and county we want to work in. Let's make this as easy as possible and select areas where we are likely to get a good response to our letters.

"As you keep getting reminded there are always exceptions to everything, but my recommendation is to find developed recreational property. As you get more into this, don't limit yourself to recreational areas, but in the beginning let's increase your odds of success.

Here are some examples, but don't feel limited to these, there are thousands more.

- Horseshoe Bend, AR..... Izard County

- California City, CA ..... Kern County

- Salton Sea, CA ..... Imperial County

- Cherokee Village, AR ..... Sharp and Fulton Counties

"The list can go on and on, but you get the idea. Even more important than whether it is recreational property or not is the ability to do extensive research online.

"Once we have decided on a county, the next step is to get a list of property owners. I have known people that just randomly mail to people who own property in a particular development. I like to be more targeted so I usually mail to property owners who were delinquent on their property taxes two or three years ago. If you want to spend a little more time, get a list from three years back, then go to the Assessor's webpage and learn if they are still delinquent. These represent all the low hanging fruit.

"Once we have the list (www.TaxSaleLists.com) sort the list down to the owners who own property in your county, but live elsewhere. They are more likely to be open to your offer.

"Now you have an excellent list to mail to. You can sort it even more by dollar value. In the beginning Dagney and I mailed to owners of property with values from $10,000 to $50,000. We mail to all of them now.

"Your greatest results will come from hand addressed envelopes with a live postage stamp. This is very time consuming. If you don't have the time to do this you can use the service at www.click2mail.com. I have had good success with them. Go to their website and look around. They offer lots of services. If you mail to a really large list, I suggest their postcards. But in the beginning I suggest you send no more than twenty letters per day. You can get overwhelmed very easily.

"Here is the letter I used for a long time:

(Author's note: There are other letters that I use with even greater success now. You can obtain a copy by requesting a copy from jimyocom@comcast.net. I never share your address and you can opt off my list at any time. Jim Yocom)

Illustration 23

I AM A REAL ESTATE INVESTOR

7/19/2007

xxxxxxxxxxxxxx

171 BELLEVILLE AVE

xxxxxxxxxx, NJ   07003

Dear: xxxxxx

I invest in real estate in Dade County, Florida . My
research turned up your name as the owner of xxxxxxxxx.
The research shows that there are taxes due.

I work with a lot of property owners that are behind on
their taxes. Usually this due to one of three reasons:

1. The property and the expenses involved have
   become a burden
2. Plans have changed since they bought the property
3. Financial circumstances have changed because of
   increased payment amounts or changes in
   employment and income

If you still have plans for the property and it has not
become a burden, you need read no further. I wish you
great good luck with your plans.

If, on the other hand your plans have changed you may find
that the solution that I have worked with others in your
situation to be attractive to you.

It is often difficult to sell property in these economic times many property owners find that the tax advantages of quickly disposing of their property to an investor actually puts more money in their pocket than a protracted sales process and high commissions paid to a real estate agent.

I am enclosing a letter from the IRS that will give you an idea of how and why this works.

If you would be open to discussing what has worked well for a lot of other people and exploring whether or not it would be advantageous to you. Please contact me.

If we can reach an agreement I can close quickly.

You can reach me at:

"Be sure to list all your contact information. If you can only be reached at a certain time of day spell that out. If it is in a different time zone explain the difference or you will get calls at midnight.

"I enclose a copy of Article 409 from IRS that we discussed previously. I highlight the paragraph that explains the $3,000 Capital Loss deduction. We usually mail letters twenty at a time, Monday thru Friday."

"I think I have a handle on everything up to this point, but what makes me nervous is selling the property on my offer when they call. What do I say?" Eric wanted to know.

"First of all let's look at this realistically. You are not going to try to sell them on anything. They have a problem or they wouldn't have called you. Often they don't want to admit to a problem or any strong desire to sell because they think it puts them in a weak bargaining position. To some extent that is true. But we aren't sending letters to try and take advantage of anyone.

"When we started we only offered $25 to everyone. That was just to compensate them for their time and effort to get the offer notarized. When someone accepts a $25 offer they are a really, really, serious Don't Wanter. Now we offer more in many cases, but still quite often our opening offer is just $25.

"You are going to learn how to offer many thousands of dollars if the property justifies it. But let's not get ahead of ourselves.

"Eric, back to what do you say when they call. You aren't making a sales presentation and you don't have a script to read. You just want to engage them in conversation. Let's just walk through an imaginary conversation.

"They will probably want to know right away what you are prepared to offer. I just say, "Well Mr. Jones, that depends on what I think I can resell the property for.

"I am a real estate investor. I don't warehouse property. I buy quickly and try to sell quickly. This makes it possible for me to offer you more money than I could if I planned to hold it for a few years. Are you okay with me making a profit?

"Sure. If I can get what I need I don't care how much you make.

"Good. Tell me, what do you need to walk away with, after the taxes are paid?"

"I'm not sure. Of course I want as much as I can get."

"We all want that don't we? Well, maybe a good place to start is to compare your property to others in the area. Do you know what other property owners around you are getting for their property?

"No. As you know I live in another state and don't keep up with what is going on there."

"According to what I find on the Internet there aren't many properties selling at all. I do know that the tax value on your property is $6,000. But if the market was good it might sell for more than that. What do you think?

"I really need to get more than that out of it."

"I understand. Tell me if we can't get together, what are your plans for the property? Will you go ahead and build on it or what?"

"No, I don't think I will ever build on it. At one time I thought I might, but not now. I guess I will just try to sell it on my own."

"How many offers have you had on this property?"

"I haven't really had an offer. I had a sign on it for a while and got a couple of phone calls, but no real offers."

"As you know there are now three years of taxes due. Evidently these are a nuisance to you. But if they aren't paid soon, the holder of the Tax Lien Certificate will foreclose. I'm not trying to paint a bad picture, but if that happens you won't get anything and you will have a foreclosure on your record."

"What is your suggestion?"

"Well if I could pay you something for your trouble in signing the papers, and you could get some money in your pocket from this property for the next few years would that appeal to you?"

"How does that work?"

"The IRS allows you to take a deduction for a capital loss on the property. So let's say, and this is just an example, if the property is worth $6,000 and I prepared all the paperwork and sent it to you along with a token payment of $25 plus the cost of getting the forms notarized, you could show a loss of $5,975. I can make up an offer and send it to you, along with a copy of the IRS rule. I would also include a Quit Claim Deed for you to sign. This will get you out from under the property completely and you won't be liable for any taxes that are due now, or in the future. Tell me where to mail these papers. You look them over and if you change your mind just tear them up and keep the $25. Fair enough?"

"This is almost verbatim of a conversation I had just recently. I finally had to pay the owner $500, in addition to the $25, but I sold it for $4,500 before I even had to pay him the $500."

"How do you sell it before you even pay him?" Allison wanted to know.

"I tell him that I think a can make a little money on the property, but since there aren't any sales in the area I need to test the market. I tell him that I am going to send him an agreement that gives me the right to try and market the property. I explain that in order to sell it the taxes need to be brought current, but for him to not worry about that because a new owner, if I can find one, will pay those taxes.

"I explain that I am going to have to advertise the property, I will need to find out the status of anything else owed on the property. All this is going to take some time and money that I will pay with no obligation to him. I hope to be able to sell it fairly quickly, but I won't know until I test the market.

"I will test the market, and if I see I can make a profit, I will give you your asking price. But in the end you don't really set the price, and neither do I. The market sets the price. Does that sound like a fair deal?

"I tell him that I will put the paperwork in the mail right away then I will call him and go over it with him.

"Every conversation will be different, but they generally fall along these lines. Just keep him talking about the property. Don't praise the property, but don't tell him it is worthless either. Just explain that in a better market and a better economy he could probably get more, but the market is very depressed right now. He watches TV and he knows that.

"Don't worry. Just get the letters out and get the calls coming in. I will help you with the first few." *(Author's note: Go to my website....... and learn how I will help you too.* Jim Yocom*)*

"Okay, I think I can do all this without any help. But, what if I do buy a property in another state. How do I sell it?" Trish asked.

"Great, Trish, you are seeing the possibilities and now you need to know how to get paid. There are lots of ways to sell the property you control, and we are going to cover several, right after a break. So take about a fifteen minute break and let's get right into the sales strategies."

Chapter 10

THE PAY WINDOW IS OPEN

"You do not need to know how things work; you need to know THAT they work"

- Author unknown

Kevin had been answering questions during the break and now he has asked everyone to take their seats.

"Okay, you have found an area where you want to work, you have sent out the letters, at least one of your offers has been accepted and now you control that property with either an Offer to Purchase or an Option to Purchase.

"Now what?"

"There are hundreds of ways to profit from properties you control or have acquired at such low costs. Here are just a few:

1. Best bet -- contact property owners on both sides of your property. They often are interested in expanding their holdings.

2. If there is enough margin, list with a local Realtor. Offer the agent an above average commission and price the property for a quick sale. You are going to

be surprised how often an agent will buy the property themselves if you offer a great price.

3. Arrange for someone, the Realtor if you list the property, to put a sign on the property with a contact phone number. If you will carry some financing, we are going to talk about that a little later, be sure the sign, and all your advertising for that matter, explains your terms. A sign that says, "Very low down payment and owner financing." will get lots of calls. Remember the story I told you about Sweetwater Hills? Roadside signs were the entire marketing program.

4. The primary aim of what we are doing is to sell the real estate without ever owning it. Or at least not owning it for more than a few days.

5. A couple of really proven ways to sell is by listing on EBay and Craigslist.

"Are you telling me that people actually sell property on EBay?" Eric wanted to know. "That seems really incredible to me."

Well, look at this next slide.

Illustration 24

"I am sorry this picture is a little fuzzy. But for those of you who are familiar with EBay, what do you notice about this screenshot of some real estate listings?"

"I shop for a lot of kid clothes on eBay so I am very familiar. Each of these properties has several bids on them." Trish answered.

"They do indeed. One of them actually has almost 40 bids. You would be amazed at the amount of real estate that is sold on the Internet.

"Would you guess that a lot of the people selling these properties got them the same way I am sharing with you? In fact I received an email from a lady a while back who was making a lot of money buying property on EBay and other sites, then marking up the price and listing them again. One fellow claims to be selling dozens of properties per month this way.

"As you know, I was in the land business for a long time. We spent a lot of money on marketing and we were very successful. Now there are land companies that are doing more business than we ever did just on the Internet. Take a look at this.

Illustration 25

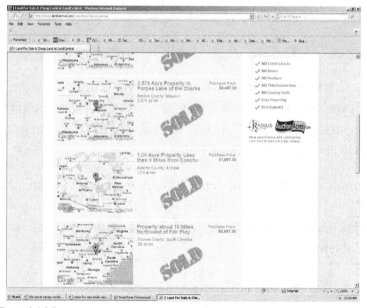

"Here's another company."

Illustration 26

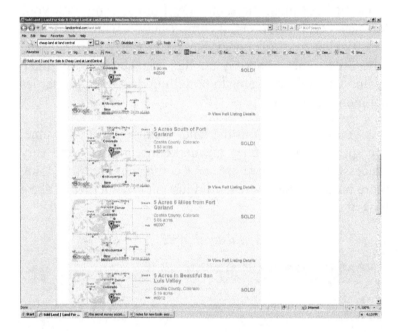

"Are you starting to see the potential in what we are doing? If you answered 'yes' you are only partially correct, because, *'YOU AIN'T SEEN NOTHING YET!'* Kevin said, in his best carnival barker imitation.

Aaron was shaking his head, "I think my head will explode. Why doesn't everyone know about this? Kevin, unless I am missing something, this could solve all of our problems."

"Yes, it can, if you will. This doesn't happen easily, but it does happen, as surely as night follows day. It is inevitable. As a matter of fact this is an excellent way to set goals. You start with the end in mind. Then decide what steps must be taken to get you to your goal.

"It is like baking a cake. You decide what kind of cake you want and assemble the ingredients that go into a cake like the one you want. Then you follow the recipe; take the steps in the exact sequence outlined. Once all the ingredients are assembled in the proper amounts in a mixing bowl and you stir them together it is absolutely inevitable that you now have cake batter.

"Now, you pour it in a cake pan, place it in an oven set at the correct temperature, set the timer for the correct baking time. It is inevitable that a cake will come out of the oven. If something is wrong, don't blame the recipe, just go back and see what YOU did wrong.

"So if you want to do one deal per month, or ten deals per month, you follow the correct steps and you are certain to meet your goal.

"You find the area where you want to work. Get your list. Send the letters. Make offers. Market the property, and if you haven't missed a step, you will inevitably meet your goal."

"This is great. Where do I get the recipe?" Allison was beaming.

"Allison, this is the reason why there aren't more people doing this. You have to make your own recipe. But you aren't starting from scratch. You know the ingredients and the sequence of steps. What you don't know is how many letters you have to send to get the number of people calling, so you can make the correct number offers, to get the correct number accepted that will lead to the correct number of deals marketed to get your one, or ten, deals per month.

"In the beginning you just experiment with the number of letters. I recommend ten to twenty per day at first. You will soon learn how many prospects this will generate. Then you will learn how many of them will accept your offer, then how many of them will be marketed successfully.

"Within sixty to ninety days you will learn the exact number. As you get more experienced, you will get more offers accepted, which will change all the subsequent numbers. But they will all change in a positive direction.

"Most people never get started. Most of the ones who start don't continue. We finally get down to the five percent who will work this as a business and all the rest will wonder, 'How did you get so rich? I am confident that you are in that top 5% or I wouldn't be spending my time with you."

Matt said, "Kevin, you can definitely count on Malone and me."

"Thanks Matt, but I don't need to count on you. You need to count on you. You are being handed a great gift, but what you do with it is just up to you. I will make you a promise right now and it comes with a silver plated, gold lined, diamond encrusted full 100% money back guarantee. You will get discouraged and want to quit." Kevin said seriously.

"No way." Aaron almost shouted.

"Just make yourself a promise. You don't need to promise me. But before you quit, or even slack off, promise that you will talk to me first. Bear in mind, I have no monetary interest in this. If you make millions, or never make a penny, I get paid the same – nothing.

"Now let's get back to business. As you know our goal on most of the properties is to get control of them and sell them before we own them. But occasionally you will want to hang on to one, and here is one of the reasons.

"A great opportunity exists for you to create a huge monthly income. Think of this. You are in the market for a new home. You see two houses setting side by side and each meets all your demands. There is a FOR SALE sign in front of each. One sign says, "FOR SALE" and the Realtor's name. The other says, "FOR SALE, OWNER WILL FINANCE -- SMALL DOWN PAYMENT AND NO CREDIT CHECK."

"Which sign will get the most calls? Yes, I think we all agree on the second sign. This brings us to a great opportunity that exists for you to create a huge monthly income.

"Offer to sell your property for a down payment and finance the balance yourself for some period of time.

"For example, you offer a lot with a Fair Market Value of $10,000 on EBay for just $5,000 or $8,000 or even FMV of $10,000. For a $500 down payment and monthly payments of $125 per month, for 36 months.

"You can arrange the terms, down payment and interest rate to suit you and your buyer. If you get $500 down on a property that you acquired for $25 you have made 20 times your original investment in cash, and will receive monthly payments for some period of time.

"You just decide how much monthly income you want and sell enough property on installment to provide it. I told you that you are in complete control. If you don't have enough monthly income, talk to the person in the mirror.

"There are several companies, such as the one in *Illustration 25* that buy large chunks of land, subdivide it and sell it just as I described. The down payment pays them for the land, the payments and interest are all gross profit."

"What if the people don't keep up their payments?" Eric wanted to know.

"You don't want to see that happen because you don't ever want to see anyone lose money, but it is a double-dip for you. You just take the property back and sell it to someone else for another down payment and new monthly payments.

"If you get serious about this business, there is no limit to what you can accomplish. There are so many ways to make money that it boggles my mind and I have been at this for a while.

"You just learned how to create a monthly income. Now, let's really learn how to make money with these strategies.

"I am going to tell you about an amazing bank. The truly amazing part comes when you learn who owns the bank.

"Let's just say you are in the market for a car. What if you saw this ad in the paper or on TV? "

NEED A NEW CAR? LET OUR BANK FINANCE IT FOR YOU.

- YOU DON'T HAVE TO MAKE A DOWN PAYMENT

- WE DON'T EVEN CHECK YOUR CREDIT

- YOU IMMEDIATELY GET A FREE AND CLEAR TITLE

- WE PAY YOU DOUBLE DIGIT INTEREST ON EACH OF YOUR MONTHLY PAYMENTS

- WHEN YOU FINISH ALL YOUR MONTHLY PAYMENTS, DROP BY THE BANK AND WE WILL GIVE ALL YOUR MONEY BACK, AND A PROFIT.

- HERE'S AN EXAMPLE. CAR SELLS FOR $20,000, FINANCE FOR 48 MONTHS AT $488 PER MONTH – TOTAL PAYMENTS=$23,4.24 AT END OF 48 MONTHS COME BY THE BANK AND TELL US WHAT TO DO. HERE ARE YOUR CHOICES:

- WE CAN GIVE YOU A CHECK FOR $35,444

- WE CAN PAY YOU $472 PER MONTH.....FOREVER!

- OR JUST LEAVE THE $35,444 IN THE BANK AND IT WILL GROW TO $689,767 IN 20 YEARS AND PROVIDE $9,196 PER MONTH IN INCOME FOREVER.....IT'S YOUR CHOICE

"Would you like to do business with that bank?

"That would be the most outlandish thing I ever heard, if it were true. Of course, there is no such bank, so what's the catch?" Matt didn't seem particularly amused with Kevin's bank story.

"Oh, but there is such a bank. There is no catch. Do you want to know who owns the bank?"

"Kevin, you are starting to make it sound as though you own a bank. Do you?" Matt frowned. "Even if you do, it can't make that offer. So who does own this mythical bank?"

"Well, yes I do own such a bank and so do you, rather you can if you want. It is up to you. We can set it up today. Then your bank can do exactly what I outlined and so much more, you won't even believe it."

"Frankly, I don't believe this." Matt still wasn't amused.

"It looks like I am in a room full of disbelievers. Does anyone believe what I just shared with you?" No one raised their hand.

"That's great. Do you remember what Lauren and I both said in the very beginning? Don't believe anything; even from us. Make us prove it. Since I am bound by my statement, I guess I had better prove what I just told you. You see, up until now, you have been assembling the tools we have given you. Now it is time to learn to use them. So let's get started."

And so Kevin began.......

Chapter 11

OF COURSE YOU CAN COLLECT INTEREST ON YOUR CAR PAYMENTS...OH YES YOU CAN!

"Success isn't created by luck. It is a formula."

- *Jim Yocom, Author*

Kevin took a deep breath, "Now follow me carefully and make notes. First of all allow me to caution you that you should never attempt this, or any tax strategy, without the help of a CPA. I am going to back up what I tell you here, but you still should consult with a tax advisor.

"I am going to use a hypothetical example here with a fictional 'Joe.' Don't try to compare Joe's situation to your own. You can make what Joe is about to do work for you but the amounts and time periods will probably vary because of different economic situations.

"Joe is going to set up a self-directed solo 401k and he is going to fund it with $40,000. Joe has a couple of sources to get his $40,000. He may roll over an IRA, or money from a 401k with his employer, or he may take out a home equity loan.

"If it isn't funded immediately, it can be done as funds are available. At any rate he sets up his self-directed 401k and at some point in time he has $40,000 in it for our illustration.

"Now stay with me here. Joe is going to invest half of his $40,000 in Tax Lien Certificates with an average interest rate of 16% from within his new 401k.

"He buys a $20,000 car with the other half.

"Joe is going to invest in these Tax Lien Certificates in resort areas. This will be on buildable lots. The taxes of most of these lots will be very small. For our illustration we will assume that taxes have been unpaid for a while so the CPs average $500 each.

"Joe's $20,000 will buy 40 CPs. Actually he could probably easily buy twice that many for $20,000.

"Joe's investments are going to follow the national averages and 3% of his CPs are going to turn to deeds. So Joe will wind up owning 1.2 properties. For this example we'll just round that off to two properties.

"Keep in mind, when I invested $1,000,000 for my friend the rate was 12% eligible for deed rather than 3%, so this is ultra conservative.

"For this amount of past due taxes these parcels will have an average FMV of around $10,000. But again, being conservative, Joe sells them for $7,000 each for a quick sale. Joe's 401k has received $14,000 from the sale of his two properties.

"The first year Joe's CPs from the original $20,000 have been earning 16% interest; $3,200. Two of them have gone to deed and he has sold them for $14,000. So there is now $37,200 in his account.

"Each time Joe makes a payment of $488, the same amount in the bank ad, back into his 401k, he buys another CP and it starts earning 16% interest.

"For this illustration I waited until Joe had made 12 payments of $488 each, for a total of $5,856, and invested it all in CPs at one time. I show it this way just to make it easier to follow. I did the same with the next three years of payments.

"Flip the calendar ahead four years. This is the value of Joe's 401k.

Joe's original investment of *($20,000 car loan now repaid)*	$40,000
His real estate profits	$14,000
Interest earned on $20K left in account	$36,212
Interest earned on Mo pmts reinvested @16%	$ 5,621
TOTAL ACCOUNT VALUE	$95,833

"This is the amount Joe will have for future investments. His earnings over the four years are $45,833. This is an annual compound rate of **28.41%.**

"I know you are writing this down so circle 28.41%. Now circle it again, and again and again.

"So where are we? At the end of four years Joe's $40,000 has more than doubled while paying for his new car at his own bank.

The rate could easily be twice or three times as much. First of all Joe would probably have gotten twice the number of CPs and the percentage going to deed would almost certainly be more than 3%. But let's be conservative and stick with the miniscule rate of just 28.41%.

"Look at what we have. Joe has set up a financial entity (a bank?) with funding (capitalization?) of $40,000. This entity is investing (loaning?) this money to earn interest.

"Let's just scratch our collective heads and see if we can think of any other entity that does what Joe just did."

"So this is how we get our bank?" Allison smiled.

"Well, if it looks like a duck, and quacks....

"Yeah, I know. If it looks like a duck, and quacks like a duck, chances are we have a genuine duck on our hands. I am naming mine 'Allison Duck National Bank." Allison laughed at her own joke and he others joined in.

Kevin cautioned, "Now we are all grown up here and we know this is not going to work out exactly like this. But all the principles will hold true. Amounts and time periods will always vary.

"By the way, in case you didn't notice, I didn't show any interest earned on the $14,000 from the real estate sale. There is no way to predict how long it would take to sell the property. Maybe one day, or maybe a year."

"Okay, I get that we each own our own bank, but I still can't get my arms around how we make the car loan you described." Malone said.

"All right, let's see if we can actually do that. Joe's 'Joe National Bank' runs the ad we talked about. The first thing the ad said was that if Joe came into the bank to finance his car there would be no down payment and no credit check; right?"

"There would be no point in checking our credit or making a down payment if we are making a loan to ourselves," Malone agreed.

"Joe is borrowing from his own bank so he will pay cash for his car and receive a free and clear title."

Trish said, "Wait a minute. This $40,000 is in a 401k right?"

"Yes," Kevin said.

"I didn't think we could take that money out until we are at least fifty nine and a half without a huge penalty."

"You are right in that you can't *distribute* the money until then. But we are talking about a *loan*. Here is what IRS says:

A 401(k) plan permits participants to take loans. The plan sets forth the loan limits of Code §72(p)(2) so that a loan to a plan participant will not be treated as a distribution to the participant. Thus, the plan provides for the appropriate dollar limit on loans, for level amortizations over no longer than five years (longer if the loan is used to purchase a principle residence), and for payments to be made at least quarterly. If a loan does not satisfy the Code's requirements, then the loan is deemed to be a taxable distribution to the participant. This can happen if the participant does not make the payments required under the terms of the loan.

"This is copied directly from the IRS website. But remember the caution. Always get professional tax help. I recommend that you use www.trustetc.com they can set up your plan and guide you through step by step. I do not get paid for recommending them, by the way.

"Now you see why I used the example of 48 month financing. If Joe is borrowing from his 401k he must pay it back within five years. I kept Joe well within the time limit.

"As Joe pays money back into the plan it is again available to reinvest so each month he can buy one or more tax lien certificates that will start earning interest.

"The way I came up with the interest from the monthly payments in the example, was to just wait until the first twelve payments were made and then invest the $5,856 at one time. So that first sum will have earned interest for three years in our example. The next year we do the same and it earns interest for two years, then the last one for one year.

"This was just for ease of illustration. In actuality I would invest monthly as the payments come in, so the earnings would be even greater.

"At the end of the four years, Joe has $95,833 in his account and all of it can earn interest at 16%. This is

$15,333 per year or $1,277 each month. So if Joe can still drive the same car for two more years his account will have earned $30,666 and just the interest will buy him a new car."

"Sometimes I wish we had never started talking about this. You are making me crazy. I am so excited, but I keep waiting for the other shoe to drop." Allison looked at Malone and Trish, "Do you feel like this, or is it just me?"

Trish smiled and said, "Every time I start having any doubt, I stop and realize that Kevin is proving every concept as we go. As he said no one would exactly duplicate this example. Some accounts might not grow as fast and others will grow faster and we have no way of knowing how many properties will go to deed. But I just ask myself. 'Can we get 16% interest on Tax Lien Certificates?' After all, if we can get the high rate of interest, everything else will certainly work. The answer is always yes. So I am OK."

"Kevin, I think the answer is obvious, but just to be sure, can we make this work with other rates of interest?" Eric wanted to know.

"Sure you can. If you get a lower rate it will take longer. If you get more it can happen quicker. What I am teaching you is a strategy, not a specific.

"While we are talking about lower interest rates I would like you to look at a very conservative scenario.

"Let's look at having $5,000 to invest in Tax Lien Certificates. Since the tax rate is generally very low on vacant land, let's assume that we buy 15 to 20 certificates.

"A little while ago I showed you a slide of properties listed on eBay. One of them was priced at $20,300 and had 42 bids on it. Do you remember it?"

Everyone nodded their heads so Kevin continued, "I looked up the taxes on this parcel and they are only $400 so by buying some for a little less, the 15 to 20 certificates are realistic.

"Our next assumption is that we are getting just 12% interest rate. The final assumption is that we get the real estate in 5% of the cases.

"Now, let's roll the clock ahead just one year. We have earned 12% interest on our $5,000; or $600. This is a fantastic rate of return. Ask your broker or banker to *guarantee* that rate for you.

"It is probably safe to assume that we are also going to get at least one piece of real estate because the people didn't redeem. In all likelihood it will probably be more.

"Based on the tax rate on the $20k parcel in the picture, our property is probably going to be worth at least $10,000, or more. Let's assume we sell it for only $5,000 to get a quick sale.

"No wait, I said we were going to be very conservative and assume that even though our property is worth $10,000, we sell it for just $3,000.

"So we have:

$ 600 from the 12% interest

$3,000 from the sale of the land

TOTAL $3,600 earnings for one year.

"We have $5,000 invested, so the rate of return on our investment is **72%.**

"But we are going to lose almost one half to taxes aren't we?"

Everyone nodded their heads, "Actually only if we choose to do so. What if the $5,000 we invested was inside a Roth IRA or something similar? Now those earnings are *income tax free FOREVER!*

"You are getting a real insiders look inside *SYNERGY STRATEGIES.* Are you seeing how all this works together?

"In the beginning I told you that I suggest you build your foundation with Tax Lien Certificates? Now you have seen that the money doesn't just have to lie there and collect interest, albeit very high interest.

"But the guaranteed rate of interest is why I like to see your foundations built this way.

"Now I just want you to let your mind wander for a few minutes, and think about how much money you could have earned in my last two examples by using Opportunity Properties rather than Tax Lien Certificates?"

"I can't think about that now, it can be so huge," Trish said.

"Yes, and no matter what happens in other strategies we will always have that firm foundation of guaranteed rates of interest to fall back on!" Malone was almost giddy.

"Okay, let's take a break and then create some money out of thin air."

Chapter 12

YOU CAN DEDUCT YOUR KIDS SNEAKERS, VIDEO GAMES, CONCERT TICKETS AND MILEAGE WHEN YOU DRIVE THEM TO SCHOOL....SURE YOU CAN!

Please understand my friend, that where you find yourself tomorrow is a function of the positive decisions and actions you take today.

- *Akin A. Awolaja*

Kevin started, "I just read that personal bankruptcies totaled 1,400,000 In 2001. This is up 19% over 2000. This means that one out of one hundred Americans are touched by bankruptcy.

"Wow!

"The article speculated about the cause of this tragedy. The consensus was that the country has been in a recession and that was the cause. No question, the economy has certainly slipped. A lot! A lot of people have lost their jobs, and that certainly is a tremendous factor.

"But what about the previous years when was no recession? There was still over 1,000,000 Americans that declared bankruptcy. In recent years employers were begging for employees. There were still a million bankruptcies. How did that happen?

"I am certainly no economics expert, but I have been dinging around with some ideas. Think about this.

"Guys do you remember when we first talked and I drew a diagram on a napkin that showed where our income goes?"

"Oh, do you mean this napkin?" Aaron asked.

"Do you mean you kept that napkin all this time?" Kevin asked.

"I sure did. Those figures really worked on me, and I have been thinking about them ever since that day. You said that equaled $1,400,000 over their lifetime.

"You said Americans averaged $35,000 per year during their working years. You also said that they pay 37% in total taxes; or $518,000 over their lifetime.

"You are on a roll here, so go ahead and share these figures again with the guys. I don't think you ladies ever saw this." Kevin said.

"Well you said we pay around 44% or $615,000 in interest over our working lives. I know these are just averages, and most households have two incomes, but it really hit home to me because Trish and I only have the one income."

"I just don't believe that 44% of our income goes to interest." Allison said.

Kevin nodded in agreement, "Frankly, yours probably doesn't. But these are government figures and they are averages. But if you look at it carefully you may be surprised. When you get home just look at your mortgage loan and car loan statements and see how much interest you are paying. Most people are shocked. In the first several years around $800 per month goes to interest on a house payment of $1,000 per month. So it adds up quickly.

"Now subtract the taxes, all your debt and interest and the $1,400,000 has dwindled to $267,000. This is just $6,675 per year, over the 40 years. This is an average of just ***$3.21 per hour! Less than half of minimum wage!!***

"Living at home and flipping hamburgers may be the best job a lot of people will ever have according to these government figures. We do need to remember that most households have two incomes, but not all, as demonstrated by Aaron and Trish.

"How do these folks make it? Part of the answer is that a lot of people depend on credit cards to stay afloat for as long as possible. The average American owes over $8,367 in credit card debt. Statistics show that most people could not pay off even half of that debt. So they make monthly payments. *To pay off just $3,000, charged to the average credit card, making minimum payments, will take 30 years.*

"On the evening news last night, there was a special segment about credit card debt among senior citizens. Their average balances have increased about 20% over the last year alone.

"The news segment cited all sorts of speculation about why this is happening. Sure, we are a great consumer society. Senior citizens aren't immune to the offerings of Madison Avenue. But, I just wonder if some, maybe most, of their credit card debt originated just to maintain their living standard.

"A lot of seniors have most of their money in certificates of deposit. Just a few years ago they could get around 10% on a five-year CD. Today five-year CDs average just 1.97% to 2.61%. If they are just living off the interest, as they should, they have had their income reduced by over 70%. Ever wonder why so many seniors are working at Burger King?

"No wonder you are all interested in how to make more money. You gotta do it. At $3.21 per hour, you aren't going to save your way to financial independence.

"So where do these folks go, and what do they do? In my personal opinion you share what you are learning. But be prepared. Almost none of them will do anything about it. They will just complain about how LUCKY you are.

"There is only one way for any of us. We can't work enough extra jobs to get to any worthwhile financial goal. We have to become a partner with our money. Regardless of how much or how little there is. You have to make your money work just as hard as you do.

"I know the question in your mind. How are you going to make $3.21 do any heavy lifting? You can't, obviously. You have to find some extra money.

"Where do you look? Willie Sutton said he robbed banks, "Because that's where the money is." You have to look where the money is. What are the two things that ate up the $1,400,000?"

"According to this sad looking napkin it is taxes and interest." Allison smiled.

"You are one hundred percent correct. So what if you could take some of that money and put it to work? If you could, somehow, have all the money that goes to either taxes or interest available to you at retirement, your future would be much rosier.

"What if you could have more money available than what you pay in taxes and interest, by just diverting some of what you are paying now, and putting it to work for you?"

"The way to save money on interest is too obvious. You have to eliminate most, or all of your debt, and incur as little debt as possible in the future.

"The greatest amount of interest, in total dollars, that most people have is on their home mortgage. What can you do about that?

"There are several schools of thought. You have to decide which is right for you.

"For example; a $200,000 house financed at 7% for 30 years will require payments of $1,330 per month. This is principal and interest only; it does not include taxes and insurance.

"Your total monthly payments will add up to $479,000. So you can see you will pay $279,000 in interest over the course of the loan.

"Some planners will tell you that if you can afford it, finance the house for only 15 years. This will require a principal and interest payment of $1,797, and total interest paid will be $123,000 or $156,000 less than the 30-year mortgage.

"Is this a good deal? It can be. A lot of people look at it as a great idea. They want to build up as much equity in their house, as quickly as possible. They are always going to need to have a place to live.

"In the event their income is disrupted because of job or health, before they have accumulated a lot of investment wealth the house can be refinanced for a source of funds. There is nothing wrong with that.

"When the house is paid off, they have eliminated that monthly payment altogether, so they can weather financial setbacks much easier.

"Others look at it this way. They want to build their empire as quickly as possible. Also, the average family moves every five to seven years. They figure they aren't going to build a huge equity in that period. They choose to take the extra $460 per month that would be required for a 15 year loan, and invest it right away.

"If they earned 16% interest on the $460 per month ($5,520 per year) for the 15-year term of the mortgage, they would have $285,160. There is nothing wrong with that.

"Which one of these scenarios is better? Either one or both. The best one is the one that you like and feel most comfortable with. The best news is that with the high interest rates that you have learned about, you have a realistic choice. With the knowledge you are learning here, and the proper research, you aren't going to lose your money, so you can make the second example absolutely work.

"Years ago I was a financial planner. Many of the people I worked with were not wealthy. They were just responsible people who were trying to get ahead in life.

"We would always spend some time discussing their financial goals. Where did they want to be in ten years, in twenty years and at retirement?

"The next step was to analyze their assets, liabilities, income and expenses. We would agree on a realistic investment rate of return, and then project where this would put them, financially, in the time periods I mentioned.

"In a great many cases, they would readily see that they were going to fall far short of their goals. In those days (I won't admit how long ago that was.) the answer was sometimes pretty simple. They needed more money, so the answer was, "Mama, you are going to have to go to work."

"That doesn't work today. Mama already works, Trish being that exception. Do you know what is sad? Mama and the entire family have to pay a tremendous price for her to work.

"For you hard working Moms, think about this. Add up all the hours that you are not available to your family because you have to work. This includes the extra time you have to spend getting ready for work, drive time to and from work and all the other activities you must do in order to have a job.

"Now take your take home pay, and divide it by these total hours. Try it. For a lot of people, this comes out to less than a dollar an hour. Regardless of your answer, it is a very high price to pay.

"I know a lot of women say they would want to work, even if they didn't need the money. I know that is true, but I have personally never met a woman, with a family, who would continue to leave the kids every day if they didn't have to. Maybe I just move in the wrong circles.

"Now what? There were only two options:

1. Increase their income

2. Decrease their expenses.

"If you are in the middle of the lake, and your boat springs several leaks, what do you do first? You have to plug the biggest leaks first because they will sink the boat in the shortest amount of time.

"From the figures I have given you, where are the biggest leaks?"

"That's easy, interest and taxes." Eric answered.

"That's right so let's start with the biggest leak: Interest. The only way to save on interest is to pay down the debt. This may take some time depending on the nature of your debt. This may also be your very best investment.

"Does it make any sense to make an investment that pays 16% if you have credit card debt that is costing you 18% to 20%? Even if you have an outstanding investment like Tax Lien Certificates that may be paying 16%, that's still less than what the impact is on your cash flow from 20% credit card debt.

"Besides, if you have a financial crisis, you can put your investments on hold. You can't put your debt payments on hold without some serious consequences.

"The first goal should be to capture as much of the fortune you will earn as possible. The second goal is to add to the fortune you will earn, by making your money work even harder than you do.

****

(From the author: *Before we go any further I need to make a disclaimer:*

Neither the publisher, author nor any representative of the publisher or the author is rendering tax, legal, accounting, or other professional advice to the reader. Readers of this material must counsel with their own personal advisors in the areas discussed herein in order to ensure proper implementation of ideas outlined herein.

The tax saving techniques that you are about to learn are real. In each case, I am including the appropriate tax codes and rulings to back up each of the techniques. But, tax law changes constantly. You need to go to your own CPA or qualified tax advisor for the exact procedures you must follow to take advantage of these ideas.)

****

"You can show your advisor the Congressional Law, U. S. Tax Code or U. S. Tax Court Ruling which specifically authorizes the deductions I am describing.

"Most tax preparers file your tax returns only with the information you give them, and do nothing more. Few of them actually give tax advice. To take advantage of the deductions you are going to learn about, you need someone who knows more than how to fill out the forms.

"If you don't already have a **_good_** CPA, get one. Then instruct your advisor that you want to take advantage of these deductions. Show the advisor the codes and rulings, and explain that you want them to advise you on the best way to proceed. You aren't asking if you *should* proceed, you are asking *how* to proceed.

"If your advisor is not fully committed to what you want, get one that is.

Chapter 13

THERE ARE TWO TAX SYSTEMS. YOU CAN CHOOSE WHICH IS BEST FOR YOU.

Most successful men have not achieved distinction by having some new talent or opportunity presented to them. They have developed the opportunity that was at hand.

"When Dagney and I needed to invest more than ever, we had no money to invest, Kevin began. "We knew about Tax Lien Certificates, Tax Deeds and Opportunity Properties but we had no way to get money to invest in any of these.

"Remember the Internet was in its' infancy then. No counties had their data on a website, so we had to travel to the counties for our research, and no money to do so. It was not possible to make a business from Opportunity Properties without any money as you can today.

"We had one very important thing going for us. We had just met Lauren so we decided to talk to her. Wow, talk about having your eyes opened! She showed us the amount of money that flowed through our account all the time. Then, wonder of wonders, she showed us how to capture some of it for our better use.

"Now you know Lauren, and I am going to ask her to come teach you what she taught Dagney and me. As you recall, most of our money goes to pay taxes and interest on various things. Lauren is going to teach you to grab this money and put it to better use.

"Lauren, would you come back up here now?"

"Thanks Kevin. Are all your heads spinning from what Kevin has taught you so far?"

Everyone agreed and Matt said, "Frankly this is what I have been looking forward to. It is so exciting to learn about all these tools and how to use them, but from time to time, we need ready cash, at least Malone and I do."

"If it is any consolation everyone does. So let's start immediately putting more money in your pocket, beginning tomorrow. Any objections to that?"

There were lots of smiles and head nodding from everyone, so Lauren began.

"What you are going to learn now can enable you to get an immediate raise in take home pay. Some of you may be able to get refunds, or additional refunds, for the taxes paid in the past three years. You are going to learn how to get future refunds in advance.

"Over the last several years our congress has eliminated many of the tax shelters that were available in time past. But, there is one shelter that has actually improved over the last few years. It is a shelter that is available to you, and even most billionaires aren't able to utilize it.

"People who trade their hours for dollars, called employees, are taxed one way, and businesses are taxed a different way. Wow, is there a lot of difference.

"An employee works and receives a paycheck. But, before the employee receives the check something has happened to it. ***Taxes have been withheld!*** The employer has been forced by the Federal Government to become their tax collector.

"Look at your last pay stub. The amount of pay you started out with doesn't look much like what you wound up with. You started with GROSS PAY. Then all the taxes come out and the difference is NET PAY. Is it really gross to look at your net?

"What you have left is all you have to pay all your expenses. Sure, you can get some tax deductions at the end of the year. You get deductions for your dependents, your mortgage interest, charitable gifts and the amount you contribute to your retirement plan. There isn't a lot more available.

"For most people these deductions don't mean anything until they file their tax returns. Then many people really look forward to a refund. A refund just means they have been making an interest free loan to the government.

"Try being late paying your taxes and see if the government grants you this same interest free courtesy.

"Let's look at a better way. A business takes in money through the sale of goods or services. They pay all their expenses ***before taxes*** and only pay taxes on what is left.

"This business probably has a lot of the same expenses that you have. A business has to pay--

- Rent or a mortgage payment
- Charitable gifts
- Insurance - health, vision, dental, property, liability, auto etc.
- Auto expense
- Newspapers
- Utility bills
- Cleaning, repairing, painting etc.
- Meals eaten away from home.
- Travel

"Do you recognize any of those expenses? Does it look like some of the same bills you pay each month? Of course there a lot more expenses that a business gets to deduct from its' gross pay. We are going to explore them in depth.

"Make sure this concept of paying before taxes, and paying after taxes, really sinks in. You pay all the expenses listed above, but you pay them with what is left over after all your taxes are withheld. At the end of the year, do you get to deduct these expenses from your taxes? Well, mortgage interest. But do you get to deduct the actual mortgage payment, or rent?

"Really? look at this. Assume you are in a 25% income tax bracket and you receive $1,000. After income taxes of $250 are withheld you only have $750. (Before all the accountants start emailing me, I know there are a lot more taxes; this is just to make a point.)

"Now, let's assume that you have to pay $500 in rent. You would have $250 still in your pocket.

"Look at a business in the same tax bracket. The business gets $1,000, pays $500 in rent, then pays 25% taxes on the other $500, or $125. Subtract this from the $500, and the business still has $375 in the till. If you have the choice between $250 and $375; which sounds best? Guess what! You have that choice.

"This is a $125 difference on just one item out of just $1,000. Starting to get the picture?

"The only difference in the two scenarios is that one is a business and one is a wage earner. Both are following the tax codes, exactly as written.

"Let's explore a little more.

"The business is in some type of building and the business pays rent. Does the IRS tell the business owner which building to rent or buy? How much to pay? Then this business could be located anywhere, couldn't it?"

Lauren smiled as she saw the lights starting to come on in the group.

"Could it be located *__in the business owner's home?__*

"Remember that the IRS doesn't tell the business owner where to locate. So, if the owner decided to locate in the owner's home, could the business take the same deductions?"

"Are you going to tell me that if I have a home based business, I can take a rent deduction?" Eric asked

"You betcha! And a lot more besides! We are just getting started."

"I don't know what kind of business I would have in my home, and if I knew how to make money with another business I would already be doing it." Allison was shaking her head.

"Don't worry," Lauren said. "I think your question about what to do will be answered in just a few minutes, so let's just take this a step at a time.

"Okay, let's take the first step to form a business that you run from your home. It doesn't matter what product or service you sell; your first step is to decide on your business structure. There are four general types of businesses, each with its' own tax considerations and protections.

"Here is some general information. Be sure and consult with your CPA and lawyer.

SOLE PROPRIERTORSHIP

"This is the easiest and most common type of business. You are the owner and perhaps the only one working the business. You cannot be an employee, because you can't hire yourself. You are liable for all costs and responsibilities and all the profits earned belong to you. You also assume all the risks.

"This is an easy way to operate a business because it requires a minimum of paper work and reporting. But I hope you heard me and were paying attention when I said, 'You assume all the risks.'

"Businesses, large and small, get sued. It is important that you protect yourself from lawsuits, whether you are at fault or not. We will talk more about this later, but bear in mind that a lawsuit could wipe you out financially even if you aren't at fault. I don't like to scare you about anything, but I want to scare you just enough to make sure you protect yourself. Generally it is so easy that anyone that doesn't take the necessary steps is very foolish.

"All income and business expense is reported on your personal income tax return on a Schedule C.

"The IRS needs a way to identify your business. If you don't have employees or file returns for employment, excise, alcohol, tobacco or firearm taxes you can just use your Social Security number. If you are subject to any of the above reporting you will need to apply to the IRS for an employer identification number.

See *IRS Publication 334: Tax Guide for Small Business*

PARTNERSHIP

"Now let's look at the second, some would say first, most dangerous form of business.

"When two or more people go into business together they go in as partners. Each partner typically contributes money, expertise etc. to the business venture.

"There is more reporting to do in a partnership than there is in a sole proprietorship. You will need an Employer Identification Number and you will be required to file an annual information return. The partnership is not taxed;

rather all income and deductions flow directly to the partners to be reported individually.

"This is the least favorable form of business ownership for a lot of reasons. Most of the reasons have to do with asset protection. Each partner is completely liable for the actions and debts of the other partner. If one partner is sued, both are sued. Over the years I have heard countless tales of woe concerning partnerships.

"I have heard hundreds of people tell how their partner was crooked, took advantage of them, was lazy etc. I have only heard from the "good" partner. I have never heard anyone say, 'I really had a great partner, but I didn't work and I took all the money.' I wonder where these bad partners go. I am sure no one has ever heard from even one of them.

See *IRS Publication 541: Partnerships*

CORPORATION

"Corporations are certainly more cumbersome than either of the two other entities we have talked about so far. But, the protection afforded all the parties certainly make it worth considering.

"Basically, when you form a corporation you have created a legal ghost. Although there is no body attached, a corporation can conduct business on its' own, incur debt, sue and be sued and all the other things that a real person can do.

"The people who form the corporation contribute certain amounts of money, goods, services, etc. in exchange for shares of the corporation. The shares are represented by shares of stock that the corporation is authorized to issue.

"The people who form the corporation are ordinarily Officers, Directors and/or employees of the corporation. This is not a requirement. You can hire outside people to manage the corporation, but in small corporations the founders are often, all three, Directors, Officers and employees. Even though you may own every share of the corporation, you are still an employee of the corporation. This carries a lot of advantages as well as disadvantages.

"First lets' get the major disadvantage out in the open. It has to do with taxation.

"There are three ways to get money out of a corporation. You can borrow money from the corporation. But if you want the IRS and maybe someday a judge, to recognize the corporation, you must borrow money from the corporation the same way you would from a bank. You need to sign a note, mortgage, mechanics lien or some other debt instrument acknowledging the debt. It must also show a repayment schedule and an interest rate. This is true even if you own every share of stock in the corporation.

"The second way to get money is to have the corporation pay you a salary. The corporation must treat you as it would any other employee. It must pay payroll taxes and all other employee related expenses.

"The third way to get money is through dividends. If the company makes a profit it can declare a dividend and distribute some, or all of the excess to the shareholders in the form of dividends.

"The problem arises if the corporation makes a profit. It must pay taxes before it can pay dividends. It reports the income and expenses on *IRS form 1120*. If the total income and total assets are under $500,000 it can report on the simpler *1120-A*. Also, even though the corporation pays taxes, your salary is subject to all the same taxes as if you were working for General Motors.

"This is a big "gotcha" in a corporation. The corporation itself must pay taxes on the profits, and then when the profits are distributed through salaries and dividends, the recipients must pay taxes again.

'The corporation must make regular payments to the IRS for payroll taxes. The corporation can make electronic deposits. Otherwise payments and a completed *Form 8109* are deposited to a specified financial institution in the area. For more information see instructions for *Form 1120-W*. For more information about corporations get IRS Publication *542: Corporations*.

"If you are going to operate as a corporation, make sure you have good legal and accounting advice. A lack of knowledge can nail you.

"The plus side is that if you are doing business correctly as a corporation and there is a lawsuit arising from the operation or debts of the corporation the lawyers can't touch you personally. The corporation shields all your personal assets.

"Any lawyer will caution you that in order to have this shield you have to do everything correctly, and in accordance with the laws of your state and the federal government.

"All your corporate records, and there can be a lot of them, must be kept up to date. If every small corporation in America was raided, and forced to produce all the corporate records instantly, probably 90% of all these corporations would be found to be illegal and all the officers and directors personally liable for everything.

"You never sign anything personally; you only sign on behalf of the corporation. Every time you write the name of the corporation you need to use the full name, including the ending: Inc., Corp. Corporation, incorporated etc. This is "to give notice to the world" that they are dealing with a corporation.

"I know from personal experience how important it is to do what Lauren is telling you." Kevin added.

"A few years ago I was sued over a matter that I am sure I would have won in court, though you never know. The best part is that the judge wouldn't even hear the case. She looked at the disputed invoice and dismissed the case without hearing it. All because I had signed the document, *XYZ Corporation, by Kevin Daniels, President.* The judge told the other party that he had not been doing business with Kevin Daniels; he was doing business with XYZ Corporation.

"The other party could have refilled the suit and named the corporation, but by now he had lost all his steam."

See *IRS Publication 542: Corporations*

<u>S CORPORATION</u>

"These are sometimes referred to as Sub Chapter S Corporations. This is a way to get all the protection afforded by a corporation without the double-tax whammy.

"An S Corp does not pay taxes. All profits and losses are passed on to the shareholders to be reported on their personal tax filings. The corporation is established as any other corporation, and then you make an IRS election for the corporation to be an S Corp.

"There are certain qualifications that must be met:

- It must be a domestic corporation
- There can only be one class of stock, not common and preferred, for example
- There can be no more than 75 shareholders. Husband and wife and their estates are treated as one shareholder
- Shareholders must be individuals or certain trusts. Another corporation cannot be a shareholder. Some tax-exempt organizations can also be shareholders
- There can be no nonresident or alien shareholders

- An S Corp cannot be a financial institution using the reserve method of accounting for bad debts
- All the shareholders must agree to the S election.

IRS Form 1120s is used to report the earnings and losses to the IRS. The corporation sends a copy of *Schedule K-1*, form *1120s*, to each of the shareholders to be used for their individual *1040* filing.

"I am not going to take the time to go through all the line by line details on these IRS documents I am giving you. It would take forever and bore us all to tears. You can read them as you need them.

LIMITED LIABILITY COMPANY

"Here is an increasingly popular form of business organization; Limited Liability Company (LLC). LLCs are fairly new; they have only been available in all fifty states within the last twelve years, or so.

The LLC is a vehicle that eliminates a lot of the problems inherent in corporations and partnerships. As we said before there is a lot of record keeping, reports and minutes of directors meetings etc. required of a corporation. If all these records are not properly done the officers and directors can be sued individually. It is called piercing the corporate veil in legalese.

"Even if all the records are correct and up to date, if the corporation is sued, oftentimes the officers and directors are also named. They are out the time and expense of proving that they are not liable.

"The LLC provides much better asset protection, because the law says that the members and managers of the LLC cannot be named in a lawsuit against the company. Many medical, legal, and other professional practices are now set up as a Limited Liability Company.

LIMITED PARTNERSHIP

"I have already given you my opinion of a Partnership, but don't confuse a regular Partnership with a Limited Partnership. This is a great business entity and has an asset protection aspect that you are going to love.

"Here are the basic differences between a General Partnership and a Limited Partnership.

- The form and legality of a Limited Partnership is controlled by state law and, of course, you must comply with every aspect of these laws. If you don't your entity will be treated as a General Partnership

- A Limited Partnership has both a General Partner, or partners, and Limited Partners. A General

Partner, usually just one, has total control of all the assets even though the actual ownership may be small

- The Limited Partners liability for debts of the partnership is limited to the amount of money actually invested in the partnership. Limited Partners have no actual say so in the operation of the partnership; this is left up to the General Partner.

"A Limited Partnership is one of the best family asset protection entities available. Income can be spread over the members of the family to lower overall tax liability.

"There is a provision in the Uniform Limited Partnership Act that you will love. It is called a "charging order." A Limited Liability company protects you personally from acts of the company. A Limited Partnership holds the partners immune from the acts of the partnership itself.

"If you are sued because of some act outside the Partnership the assets you have conveyed to the Limited Partnership is protected.

"If a creditor gets what is called a charging order against the assets you have in the Limited Partnership he cannot force the Limited Partnership to give up those assets. Here is the best part; the creditor is allowed your share of the income distribution of the Partnership, but he cannot force the Partnership to distribute income.

Also while he has the charging order, the Partnership continues to operate and make a profit and pay taxes. EVEN THOUGH THE CREDITOR GETS NO MONEY HE IS LIABLE FOR HIS SHARE OF TAXES THAT THE PARTNERSHIP MUST PAY!

"Score one for the good guys. If he can't get the money but has to pay taxes, how often do you think a Limited Partnership is sued for the assets of a partner?

"Let's roll the clock ahead and assume you now have a home based business, or you have decided to start one. You have chosen the legal entity for your business. You need to convert as many of your home and living expenses as possible to business expenses.

"Before we do that let's make sure you understand what this is all about.

- First of all a legitimate home based business does not increase the likelihood of an audit. Unless you are doing something outrageous such as claiming huge expenses year after year, while producing no income, you stand no greater risk of an audit than anyone else does. Even if you are audited you have nothing to fear as long as you have the proper documentation. You are going to learn how to properly document everything.

- Many people, including a lot of tax preparers, believe that you must make a profit in three out of five years in order to deduct your business expenses. They are confusing a *hobby business* with a legitimate, for profit business. If you build birdhouses as a hobby and sell one from time to time, this is a hobby business.

- If you meet the criteria you are going to learn and actually start producing birdhouses commercially, this is a legitimate business and the three-of-five rule does not apply.

"How many years did Amazon.com lose money? It was several years before they showed a profit. Do you think they deducted their legitimate business expenses?

"A lot of people believe that in order to deduct expenses associated with a home based business they must have an area, or a room, that is exclusively devoted to the business. If you have a product to sell and can display them in different parts of the house and these are identifiable spaces you can add up this identifiable space and claim that as a business deduction.
    (IRC) § 280 A(c)(2)

"How do you make sure you qualify? First, be sure you have a CPA who is knowledgeable of home based business. You must demonstrate your profit making intent. More about this later. Then you must regularly conduct your business from your home.

"You just need to show that your home is your regular place of business and you conduct business on a regular basis from your home.

"I have heard so called "EXPERTS" say that you can only deduct home based business expenses up to the amount the business earns. This only applies to a category called "Indirect Expenses." This is a small part of your total deductions, and even these deductions can be carried forward from year to year until they are all used.

"If you have formed an LLC, for example, all the business expenses are deducted directly on your personal taxes.

"You must set up your business from the very beginning just as you would if you were starting a business in another location.

"You need, actually must have, a business checking account. Register your business name or incorporate. If possible use a separate credit card to pay business expenses that are not paid by a business check. I don't want another credit card, so I have a Visa Debit Card that is strictly for business.

"If you are required to pay sales tax, get a sales tax license and post it in your business. If you need a business license get one. In other words you actually must have a legitimate business in order to qualify for the tax deductions. Just signing up for a multi-level marketing program, not really working it and saying you are in business won't work. The deductions are for legitimate business expenses, including multi-level marketing, if done correctly.

"The primary consideration of whether a home based business qualifies for business deductions, is the owner's

"Intent to make a profit." The IRS has eight primary, though not exclusive, factors they consider. You need to be aware of them.

IRS Regulation 1.183 (b)

At this point Lauren handed everyone a sheet with the requirements IRS recognizes for a home based business.

She said, "Here are eight points that IRS looks for to establish that a home based business is legitimately in business. The most important point is to spell out in the very beginning that you are in business to make a profit.

"In the by-laws of a corporation spell out that the business is formed for the purpose of creating a profit for the benefit of the shareholders.

"Let's look at these requirements.

EIGHT REQUIREMENTS FOR A HOME BASED BUSINESS

1. *The manner in which the taxpayer carries on the business activity.* This simply means the taxpayer carrying on the affairs of business the same as if the business were located in an office building with lots of employees. You should have a business plan and try to follow it as closely as possible. Keep phone records to show that you are making business calls during most days.

2. *The time and effort expended by the taxpayer in carrying on the activity.* Keep receipts for office

supplies, phone bills, printing bills etc. These shouldn't all be in one day per month. If they are spread out it shows that you are pursuing your business activities on a regular basis.

3. *The expertise of the taxpayer or his advisors.* If you know nothing about airplanes, but you claim your business is brokering the sale of airliners, you need to have some experts on board, or available, that act as your advisors. You don't need to be an expert; you just need to show that you have the expert help available.

4. *The expectation that assets used in the activity may appreciate in value.* This is very subjective. Not all assets appreciate, in fact few do. This is only one factor, so don't let this worry you. Nobody expects a computer you buy for your business today to be worth more in three years.

5. *Success of the taxpayer in carrying on other similar or dissimilar activities.* Here again this is very subjective. If you have ever had any experience in something even remotely similar to your new business endeavor you meet the test. It doesn't mean that if you decide to set up an Internet business that you have to prove that you have run an Internet operation in the past. You should show that you have expert help available.

6. *Taxpayer's history of income or loss with respect to the activity.* If you run the same business for a

number of years and it loses money every year, and shows no sign of improvement, you could have some serious conversation in an audit. If the original business isn't successful, switch to another business and everything starts all over.

7. *Amount of the occasional profits.* Your business needs to be bringing in some money at some point in time. Otherwise, the IRS may assume that your intention is not to make a profit at all. That doesn't mean you have to make sales your first day. Maybe even the first year, depending on the business. Just be real, and run a real business.

8. *Elements of personal pleasure or recreation.* In all you do, try to think like an auditor. If you, in your auditor hat, look at a taxpayer that routinely deducts expenses such as, expensive meals, fishing trips, and all the expenses related to playing golf, would you wonder if this person is really in business, or is just acting like it in order to deduct these pleasure expenses?

"This sounds so hard. Is this really necessary, and is the effort worthwhile?" Allison was rubbing her temples.

"Only if you need more money than you can readily take out of your budget in order to make this all work," Lauren said.

"Even if extra money to invest is not a problem it is still the prudent thing to do. Why would you want to send the government more money than you have to? We certainly caution everyone to pay their taxes, but we needn't pay one penny more than is due.

"Okay it does take some effort. Is the effort any different than what you would have to do in any other type of business? No. How much time will be required? If you set everything up correctly from the beginning, only a few minutes a day.

"Is an extra $500 or so in your pocket each month worth the effort? You tell me. What happens if you invest this $500 per month in Tax Lien Certificates, Tax Deeds, or Opportunity Properties? You already know the answer.

"You have a legal right to be in business and to take all the legal tax deductions that have been made available through the U. S. Congress.

"We have talked about the need to document that you are in business to make a profit. One of the easiest ways to do this is by having a written business plan. The plan doesn't have to be lengthy. You can follow the outline provided in the back of this book.

"You need to set up a separate checking account for your business. All money received by the business should be deposited in this account. Don't deposit business receipts in your personal account. All company related expenses should be paid out of this account. You need to keep the receipt for payment as well as your cancelled check.

"You should rarely pay cash for anything. There is no paper trail with cash, and a paper trail is what you will need in an audit.

Your first goal should be to convert as many personal expenses as possible to business expenses. IRS is obligated to collect every penny of taxes that you owe. There are federal laws that require them to do so. There are also laws that allow you to take certain legal deductions.

"The government is not obligated to inform each taxpayer of these deductions. It is your obligation to yourself and your family to be familiar with them and take the maximum deductions allowed. All the information is available on www.irs.gov.

Chapter 14

IT'S TIME TO GET SERIOUS ABOUT YOUR MONEY

Risk comes from not knowing what you are doing.

- *Warren Buffett*

-

Lauren began, "Let's talk about how we can save money on certain taxes. Bear in mind we are talking about legitimate deductions. No one wins, in the long run, by taking risky deductions. Know what you are doing, then go full steam ahead.

"All of you are taking notes and that is great. I just want you to keep in mind that all the strategies and deductions I am sharing with you, are for this day. Tax laws and rulings change almost daily. What is a legitimate deduction that I tell you about today, may not be allowed tomorrow. Work closely with your CPA.

"Here are some of the deductions available to a business:

- Security alarms
- Phone bills
- Lawn maintenance
- Health care premiums

- Water, electricity and gas
- Auto expense
- Travel expense
- Retirement plan contributions

"The list could go on and on. The point is this; do any of these expenses look familiar? Aren't they the same expenses that you are now paying?

"The goal is to convert as many of these personal expenses to business expenses as we can. Let's start with ---

BUSINESS TAX STRATEGY NUMBER ONE

AUTOMOBILE

"If you are using your automobile in your business to any extent at all, this will represent a major deduction. You have a choice of two ways that you can claim your deduction. *(Rev. Proc. 94-73) (IRS temp. Regs, §1.274-5T(B)(6)(b))*

1. You are allowed to deduct 51 cents per mile that you use your car in your business, or
2. You can deduct the actual costs of owning and operating your automobile multiplied by the percentage that your business use is to the total use. In other words take the lease payment or depreciation, repairs, tires, gas, oil, insurance, registration, etc. and multiply this figure by the percentage of the miles you actually used the car in business. For example, if you use your car

50% for your business, you multiply the total operating expense by 50% to find the amount you are allowed to deduct. *(Rev. Proc. 94-73)*

"For most people it is easier to just keep track of the business mileage and multiply that by 51 cents. *(the 51 cents is for 2011)* Use the business log found in the back of this book. Keep this one as an original and make copies.

"In either case you must maintain the mileage log. This is used to determine the percentage of total miles, your business miles represents.

"What constitutes business use? It can be a number of things. For example:

- Sales calls
- Trips to the bank for business purposes
- Trips to the office supply store
- Trips to the post office
- Trips to the court house to research properties
- Business trips to buy Tax Lien Certificates, Tax Deeds or to do research on properties.

"These are just examples. Any use of your car associated with a business purpose is tax deductible.

"If you have a home based business, as we are suggesting, almost everywhere you go can be business related. Some home based businesses lend themselves to this better than others.

"For example, if you are selling a product or service to the general public, some will tell you that if you talk to someone about your business or hand out a card or brochure while you are there, your trip to the grocery store is tax deductible.

"Before you take this deduction, discuss this with your accountant. This is an example of why you must have an accountant that is *very* familiar with home based businesses. Our job is not to tell you what to deduct. We will give you examples of deductions that some people claim, but check with your *knowledgeable* accountant.

"The test that determines whether the trip is tax deductible is the primary purpose of the trip. If your primary purpose is to buy milk and bread and you just talk to someone in line at the checkout counter, the trip is not deductible.

"But what if the primary purpose of the trip is to check your mail at the post office? If you have a business mail box, the trip is clearly deductible. What if the grocery store is on the way to the post office? You can stop on the way as an incidental part of the trip, and still take the deduction

"Do you drive the kids to school? Is your post office or office supply store, or bank on the other side of the school from your house? Starting to get the picture?

"Just from these examples, you can see the importance of planning. You want every deduction that you are entitled to, but don't make the mistake of trying to claim more than that. A little planning will result in thousands of dollars in your pocket at the end of the year.

"You can deduct tolls and parking fees if it is connected with your business.

(Rev.Proc. 90-59, I.R.B. 1990-52 § 4.04)

"Do you mean to tell me that I can deduct the mileage I drive taking the kids to school?" Trish asked.

"No you can't. But if you have to make a stop at your business mail box, an office supply store or bank; that trip is deductible. If the school is on the way, that is incidental. Even if you have to drive a few blocks out of the way to drop off the kids, it is still worthwhile. I would just figure the distance from my route to the bank that is required to get to the school and back to my bank route and not deduct that amount.

"Always, always, always clear this with your accountant. If the accountant says you can't do it and the tax code says you can, get another accountant.

"The IRS requires you to furnish the following proof. *(IRC § 274 (d))*

1. Total miles driven during the year
2. Total miles driven for business use
3. Date of mileage and expenses
4. Where the miles were driven
5. The reason for the business use

(Author's note: Look at the log example in the back of this book and you will see that the records are easily maintained. You just can't afford to not keep good records. The IRS requires you to keep good records just as it does for major corporations.)

"The IRS has ruled that even if you only keep records of mileage for part of the year, you can use that as a basis for calculating mileage for the entire year.

"However you do have to be able to prove that your representation is correct.*(Reg. § 1.274-5T ©(3)(ii)(A))*

"It is much easier to just keep a complete mileage log for the entire year.

BUSINESS TAX STRATEGY NUMBER TWO

DON'T EVER TAKE ANOTHER VACATION!

"No, I am not telling you that you should work 365 days a year. You need time to relax and enjoy vacations with your family. But instead of a vacation, take a business trip.

"Can your home based business benefit from trips to various locations? Once you are buying and selling enough tax deeds etc. to qualify as a legitimate business there is really no limit to where you might go to research property, attend an auction or just check on property that you own.

"Is a total vacation for your family for two weeks going to be tax deductible? No. But the actual business portion of the trip can be tax deductible.

"There are certain qualifications and restrictions that you need to be aware of. Here are some.

- IRS allows you to deduct travel expenses when your business requires you to sleep or rest away from wherever your principal place of business is located. *IRC § 162(a)(2)* If your business is in your home, this is literally any time you travel away from home. *Rev.rul. 54-497:75-432; 63-145;75-169; 76-453*

- There is a three-part test you must meet to determine if your trip is going to pass muster.
  1. Is the trip appropriate and helpful to your business?
  2. Is it customary within your industry for people to take such trips?
  3. Is the trip taken with the intent of obtaining a direct business benefit?

- You may deduct the cost of your travel and once you are at your destination you may deduct other expenses such as meals and lodging. Even if your trip does not include enough business days to be a legitimate business trip you can still deduct food and lodging. *IRC § 162(b)(1)*

- Okay, what is the rule to determine if your trip is business or personal? You must spend more days on business than you spend on personal pursuits to qualify as a business trip. This is the 51/49% test. If you spend 51% of your time on business the entire cost of the trip is tax deductible. *IRC § 1.162-2(b)(2)* The primary purpose of the trip still has to be business related. If you took a three-day trip and only spent one day on business and the other two on personal pleasure you would lose your travel deduction. You can still deduct the food and lodging for the one business day only.

- You can deduct weekends and holidays if they fall in between the business days. For example if you arrive at your destination on Thursday, and will not conclude your business until the following Tuesday, the expenses for the weekend are deductible. This is assuming that you are at a destination that makes it impractical to return home for the weekend. *Reg § 1.274-4(d)(2)(v)*

- Most of the time you can save money on an airline ticket if you stay over a Saturday night. If this is the case, you can count Saturday as a business day. *PLR 9237014*

- Travel days are counted as business days if the travel time is at least four hours. The time includes the time spent traveling to the airport, waiting on your plane, and the time required to get to your hotel when you reach your destination. With some of the new security precautions, it might take four hours at the airport alone. Even though your schedule does not provide time to actually conduct business, all your business related expenses are deductible. *Reg. § 1,274-4(d)(2)(I)*

- It doesn't matter how you travel, coach or first class, plane, boat, train or your personal automobile. You could even charter a private plane, the expense is still deductible to your home based business the same as the executives of large multinational corporations. *IRS Pub. 463.* Okay, there is an exception. If you travel on a yacht or cruise ship, your deductions are limited to the highest amount allowed the executive branch of the government, when traveling in the contiguous United States. *IRC § 195(b)(1)*

"You have the same deductions that the President of the United States or the President of General Motors has. I told you this home based business was a really great idea.

- What if you travel to another state to attend a Tax Deed sale and take your family along? The primary purpose of the trip is business related, so your expenses are deductible. Food and lodging costs are not deductible for your family. Just subtract the cost of the family's food and extra cost of lodging and deduct the rest. If you spent a total of four days driving to and from your destination, one day researching property, another day at the auction and took your family sightseeing for two days, you would still meet the 51/49% test, and the trip would qualify for a deduction.

- Travel expenses for your spouse is ordinarily not tax deductible. However, as in most things with the IRS there is an exception. In this case there are at least three exceptions. *IRC § 274(m)(3)*

1. The spouse or other companion is your business employee
2. The spouse or other companion is along for a bona fide business purpose
3. The travel expense of the spouse or others would ordinarily be tax deductible.

- What about your laundry and dry cleaning while on a business trip? As long as the business trip is the reason that the clothes need laundry or dry cleaning the cost is deductible. You can get the services done while on the trip, or after you get home.

The usual expenses incurred in travel on business are deductible. They include:

1. 50% of meal cost *Reg. § 1.162-2(a)*
2. Lodging and all transportation costs *IRS Pub.463 Travel & Entertainment*
3. Operating and maintenance expense of vehicles *IRS Pub.463 Trav & Ent*
4. Cleaning and laundry *Rev. Rul. 63-145, 1963-2 C.B. 86*
5. Telephone expense *Reg. § 1.162-2(a)*
6. Cost of a stenographer or dictating equipment *Reg § 1.162-2(a)*
7. Cost of transportation to the airport and back on your return. Also the cost to and from airport to your hotel or meeting place, and from one business

meeting place or sales call to another. *IRS Pub. 463 Travel & Entertainment*

8. Tips, usual and customary, for above expenses. *IRS Pub. 463 Trav & Ent*

"Okay, these are all legitimate deductions if you qualify for them. How do you qualify? Document all your expenses. Do it as you incur the expenses. Keep all receipts for all expenses. *IRC § 274* If you write the expenses down at the time you won't forget them. Also IRS says that you have a higher degree of credibility.

Reg § 1.274-5T©(1)

"Keep a diary and record everything. At the end of the day put all the receipts, along with your written record in one place. You need to record: *Temp Reg § 1.274-5T(b)(2)*

"You need to record:

- Record the amount you spend on each item. You can lump them into categories such as meals, gas, tips etc.
- Keep a record of when you leave on a trip, when you return to validate the number of days.
- Record the destination. *Temp Reg § 1.274-5T(b)(2)*
- Record the purpose of the trip; sales calls, convention, Tax Auction etc.

"You need to keep receipts for your motel along with any other expenditure of $75 or more. A great habit to develop is to keep a receipt for everything.

BUSINESS TAX STRATEGY NUMBER THREE

BUSINESS ENTERTAINMENT AND MEALS

"You can deduct legitimate business meals and entertainment, but do it correctly. Entertainment is broadly defined. It can be expenses for business socializing at sporting events, theatres, cocktail lounges etc. It can also be trips for hunting, fishing etc. *Reg. 1.274-2(b)(1)(I)*

"Once again we get back to documentation. I can't over emphasize how important it is to get in the habit of writing everything down and keeping a receipt. It only takes a few seconds when you incur the expenses, but over a year of time the deductions can be very significant. Here are the requirements:

1. Record the amount of each expense. You can total the small amounts at the end of each day and you do not need a receipt. *Reg 1.274-2(b)(1)(I)* For expenditures over $75 per transaction you need to write them down and keep a receipt. *IR-95-96; Reg 1.274-5T(c)(2)(iii)(B)*

2. Record the date of the expenditure or the date you paid for the use of a facility, such as a hotel meeting room, for entertainment. If the entertainment is just before or just after a business discussion record how much time you spent on the business discussion. *Reg. 1.274-5(b)(3)(ii)*

3. Record the place where the entertainment took place and where the business discussion took place. Show the date and time that the business discussion took place. *Reg. 1.274-5(b)(3)(iii)*

4. Record the business reason and what business benefits you were trying to gain as a result of the entertainment and business discussion. *Reg.1.274-5(b)(3)(iv)*
5. Record the business relationship you have with the person or persons entertained. *Reg. 1.274-6(b)(3)(v)*

"The IRS has two tests they use in determining whether your meeting and entertainment qualifies for tax deduction. You must meet one of the two.

- Directly related tests: To qualify for a tax deduction the expenditure must meet the four-requirement test, or the event must occur in a clear business setting.

  1. You must have had more than a general expectation of a future benefit at the time you committed to spend the money.
  2. During the entertainment, you actively discussed the topic that could produce a future business benefit.
  3. Your principal reason for the activity was the active conduct of your business.
  4. You incurred the expense to speak with the person who produced your general expectation of future business benefit.

"Could a round of golf and a meal at the club qualify? Yes. You are in an environment that is conducive to business discussion. And before you ask, the golf game that got this all started won't qualify," Lauren smiled.

- Clear business setting: You don't have to meet these four requirements if there was a clear business setting where the meeting and entertainment took place. The IRS says that in this case the entertainment is deductible as "directly related entertainment." This happens when:

  1. The person with whom you have the business discussion knows you are spending your money on the entertainment to directly further your business.
  2. You spend your money in a hospitality room at a convention where you display your products to further your business.
  3. You have no meaningful social or personal relationship with the people with whom you have the business discussion.

"If you go to a rock concert, or noisy nightclub where there is little opportunity to reasonably discuss business, IRS is not going to allow this to pass muster. For "directly related entertainment" to qualify the meeting must take place in a setting where you could reasonably carry on a business conversation.

"Some of the places that would not qualify under the Business Setting rules could very well qualify under "Associated Entertainment."

- Associated Entertainment: You may be able to deduct *indirectly* associated entertainment if you can meet a couple of requirements.

  1. The entertainment must be associated with the active conduct of your business
  2. The "associated entertainment" must be just before or right after the entertainment and you must DOCUMENT it.

"If you go somewhere that is not conducive to a business discussion, a ball game for example, but immediately after the game you take your business guests to a restaurant for dinner and a bona fide business discussion. Then the dinner expense is deductible under the Clear Business Setting rule and the ball game could be deductible under the rules for Associated Entertainment. If you qualify you could deduct 50% of the cost of the meal and entertainment.

"In your documentation, you should explain why the entertainment was associated. Then explain the purpose of the business meeting in the restaurant and generally what was discussed. It is a good idea to also include comments as to what you expect to gain from the meeting.

"If you are attending a networking meeting with business prospects, and you include an actual sales presentation, either by yourself or by a speaker to your group, this can be 100% deductible.

"As I said earlier, before in incur any entertainment expense that you want to deduct, look at the activity through the eyes of an IRS auditor. If someone plays golf with the same bunch of cronies every week, would you allow that deduction if you were an auditor? Probably not. In most businesses, this is one of the smaller items of deduction, so be cautious. Don't risk a closer scrutiny of your returns just in order to save a few bucks in this category.

"As long as there aren't any unusually large deductions, none of this will probably raise a flag. But you can't be too careful in case you get an overly ambitious agent."

BUSINESS TAX STRATEGY NUMBER FOUR

HIRE YOUR FAMILY MEMBERS

"Do you have a spouse and/or children at least six years old? Of course I already know the answer, but just go along. Let's look at the kids first.

"Do your kids ask for money for?

- Concert tickets
- Video games
- Expensive "Air Somethingorother" sneakers
- School supplies
- School trips
- Clothes
- How about your daughter's wedding

"The list could go on forever. Can you take a tax deduction for all this plus school lunches? Don't be too quick with your answer. This can be one huge advantage of having a home based business. You **_can actually deduct the cost of all these items and a lot more._**

"Is there a line on your 1040 to deduct a concert ticket to see a LADY GAGA concert? Well, not exactly, but there is a line on your *Schedule C Profit or Loss From Business.* Item number 26 *Wages* is the place to enter these deductions. This requires a little explanation.

If you had a business located in a building other than your home, could you deduct the cost of janitorial services, how about packing and shipping, what about addressing or stuffing envelopes? If you are going to hire someone to perform these services, does the IRS tell you whom to hire? Could you hire a family member? How about one of your children?

"You probably already have your kids doing a lot of this work right now. Instead of giving them an allowance, why not hire them and pay them a salary. The salary is tax deductible and they can then buy their own "Air somethingorother" sneakers and concert tickets. Same amount of money, but allowances aren't tax deductible and wages are.

"As you have learned to anticipate there are certain rules and guidelines that must be observed.

"First of all the child must be a bona fide employee over the age of six. *Eller vs Commr. 77TC 934;Acq. 1984-2 C.B. 1* If the child is at least six but under eighteen they are exempt from payroll taxes. *IRC §§3121(b)(3)(A);3306(c)*

(5) you can deduct their wages under the following rules. *Reg. § 1.162-7(a):*

1. The wages must be reasonable in amount. You can't pay one of your children $20 per hour to take out the trash. But, you could pay them $25 per hour to program your computer, because programmers in your area make that much.
2. There must actually be services rendered by the child to earn the wages.
3. The wages are actually paid, and are consistent. The best way is to pay your children by check and for them to deposit it in their own bank account.
4. You have to complete the required federal and state payroll tax and W-2 forms.

"This strategy is only useful if you are a sole proprietor, have an LLC, an S Corp or some other entity where expenses flow directly to you personally.

"If you have a C corporation, the corporation can hire the kids and take a deduction, but you can't deduct the wages on your personal 1040.

"What if the kids are over eighteen? You can still pay them for their actual services, but you must report and pay all payroll taxes. If they are in a lower tax bracket than you, this can still be very advantageous.

(Authors Caveat. *You need to read this entire section and consult with your CPA, who is well versed on taxes as they apply to home based businesses, before you begin to take any of these deductions.)*

"You are hiring your children to perform jobs that would otherwise seriously eat into your time, or force you to hire someone else. This way you get a tax deduction, the same as if you hired someone outside the family. But, you don't have to pay social security and Medicare taxes. This saves you over 15% immediately. *IRC §§ 3121(b)(3)(A); 3306(c)(5)*

"If your children have no more than $250 of unearned income, such as interest, they have to pay no income tax on more than $4,000 of income that you pay them. The amount they can earn varies each year, but is usually the same amount as the standard deduction for a single filer. *Rev. Proc. 95-53, IRC § 63(h)(2)*

"If your child is a whiz computer programmer, or have a lot of shipping that they handle you may wind up paying them more than the non-taxable amount. But you only pay taxes on the excess amount and recently that beginning rate was 15%. *Rev.Proc.95-53.12*

"Be sure and check with your local CPA about state taxes.

"Now that your children are earning wages rather than receiving an allowance, you are able to deduct the amount you are paying them.

"What can they do with the money after you pay them? If you hired someone outside the family, what could they do with the money you paid them? Anything they please. They could buy concert tickets, video games, CDs, Air

Somethingorother sneakers etc. Your children can do the same thing.

"As I mentioned before the children should have their own bank account. Since they are minors the account will have to be a joint account with you, and you will actually have to be the one signing the checks.

"Here is what it might look like. Assume that you earn $60,000 from your home based business. You have three children between six and eighteen years old. You pay each of them $350 per month to help you in your business. This is a total of $12,600 in wages that you would deduct on Schedule C.

"You deduct the $12,600 from your $60,000; this saves you $3,528 on your federal income taxes of about 28% and another $1,890 savings on over 15% employment taxes. It is all the same amount of money coming in from the business and about the same amount going out to the kids. But because it is wages and not allowances there is $5,418 more money in the family.

"The kids can buy their own school clothes and lunches and your daughter can pay for her own wedding out of the tax deductible dollars they receive and you get huge tax savings. This is equivalent to getting an increase of $451.50 per month in actual "take home" pay.

As always get your CPA, who is familiar with home based businesses, to help you set this up and document it.

"Here is another area where you need to put on your IRS auditor hat. Rest assured when they see that you are paying wages to your children they are going to look at this very closely. Perhaps closer than your other expenses. Don't let this scare you. The deductions are legitimate as long as they are properly documented. Here are some steps to take, but you should take these steps no matter who you hire.

1. Ask your CPA to help register you as an employer with federal, state and local authorities
2. Make sure you have all the necessary employment forms: Employment application, W-4, I-9 etc.
3. Write out a job description describing the work to be done and the rate of pay, hours etc. It doesn't have to be a long description. You should check around to find out what similar jobs in your area pay. Make a record of your research. An easy way to do this is to contact an employment agency, explain your job requirements and get three quotes.

"You will need a federal employer identification number (FEIN). You can obtain a federal form SS-4, Application for Employer Identification Number, these forms are available on the IRS Internet site, www.irs.gov or you can call 1-800-tax-form.

"You will also need a time sheet and your children need to record the hours worked and the work performed just as you would require from any other employee. You will find a sample time sheet at the back of this manual, or you can purchase them at your local office supply store.

"As an employer you are required to maintain certain employee records regardless of who your employees are. You need a file for each employee that contains:

- Federal W-4 Employee's Withholding Allowance Certificate
- State W-4 form or state equivalent, if required
- Federal I-9
- Job description, including hours required, holidays, amount of overtime pay if necessary
- Record of how you arrived at the payroll amount
- Employment application (You can get these from any office supply store.)
- If you provide any fringe benefits you need to have a complete description of these benefits in the file.

"Is this starting to sound like a lot of work? It really isn't. The employee files are done once, and then you are through. You need the weekly time sheet, and you need to pay by check. Not much work, for such a big payoff. Be sure and have your CPA who is knowledgeable of home based businesses help you.

"Take a look at this and decide if it is worth some extra effort.

1. Take your children off your personal tax returns, because they are no longer dependents. *IRC Sec. 127(b)(3)*
2. Have the children file their own tax returns. They are entitled to the standard deduction, and their personal exemption. *IRCSec63©(2)Rev.Proc.97-57* and *IRCSpec 151(d), Rev Proc. 97-57*
3. Each child can establish its own IRA, *IRC Sec/408(a).Reg/ 1/408(b). Publication 17* and make regular contributions. *Notice 82-13*
4. As the employer, you can now pay certain wages to each child under 19 free of Social Security taxes, Medicare taxes, Federal unemployment taxes, or Federal income taxes. *Pub. 15(Circular E), Sec 3, Pg 10*
5. You can set up a deferred compensation plan as a Simple retirement account contribution into the IRA of each child. The amount changes in some years, check with your CPA. Plus the business can match up to 3% of the child's contribution. *IRC Sec.408(p), Notice 98-4*
6. You can pay up to $5,250 for education expense for each child, and the payment is excluded from the gross income of the employee; your child. *IRC Sec. 127(a)(2),(b),(c); Reg. 1.127-2*
7. The child can use this money to pay for college and not be subject to the early withdrawal penalty

"These benefits could easily add up to as much as $20,000 and save over $5,000 in income taxes while establishing a college fund.

BUSINESS TAX STRATEGY NUMBER FIVE

WHAT ABOUT OTHER FAMILY MEMBERS?

"Okay, hiring the kids is great, what about your spouse? Could you get similar benefits from hiring him/her? Certainly! Could your spouse go back to school to get a degree, or an advanced degree and make the tuition tax deductible? It works for the kids; it will work for your spouse.

"Another caveat; if you offer this to one employee you must offer it to all of them. If you have employees, other than family, you may want to take a closer look at this. *IRC § 162-(a)*

.

BUSINESS TAX STRATEGY NUMBER SIX

BUSINESS USE OF YOUR HOME

"So far we have talked about a lot of different tax deductions that are available to you because you have a business based in your home. As you have seen this can save thousands of dollars each year that previously had been going to the government.

"We first started talking about a home based business because we were looking for additional money to invest. Since taxes are the largest drain on your income, this is where we started to look for ways to divert some of the money into Tax Lien Certificates, Tax Deeds, Struck Off Properties and Opportunity Properties.

"Now we are going to discuss the business use of your home itself. This is an area that is misunderstood by most people. I have found a lot of tax preparers that did not understand how to take the legitimate deductions that we are going to discuss now.

"The Internal Revenue Service says, "To deduct expenses related to the business use of part of your home, you must meet specific requirements. Even then, your deduction may be limited. To qualify to claim expenses for business use of your home, you must meet the following tests.

"Your use of the business part of your home must be:
a. Exclusive (however, see Exceptions to Exclusive use later).

b. Regular

c. For your trade or business, AND

1. The business part of your home must be ONE of the following:

a. Your principal place of business (defined later).

b. A place where you meet or deal with patients, clients or customers in the normal course of your trade or business, or

c. A separate structure (not attached to your home) you use in connection with your trade or business." *IRS Publication 587, Business Use of Your Home (2001)*

"It doesn't matter if the home is owned or rented. A home is defined as, "a house, apartment condominium, mobile home, or boat." Yep, you read it right; it can even be a boat. Does this bring visions of conducting your business from your tax-deductible yacht? Naah, you wouldn't want to do anything like that. Would you?

EXCLUSIVE USE

"To qualify under the exclusive use test, you must use a specific area of your home ONLY for trade or business. The area does not need to be marked off by a permanent partition, but it must be identifiable as a separate area.

"The IRS uses an example of an attorney working at home to illustrate what does not qualify. If the attorney uses the den to write legal briefs, etc. but your family also uses the den for recreation, it clearly does not qualify.

EXCEPTIONS TO THE EXCLUSIVE USE

"You do not have to meet the Exclusive Use rule to qualify for a deduction. If you use your home for storage of inventory or product samples, or you use part of your home as a day-care facility, you qualify.

"If you store products in one half of your basement, you can still take a deduction for that space even though you do not use this part of your basement exclusively for business.

"If you display products in various places in the house this space is also deductible. For example, if you display products on a coffee table, the square footage of the table, plus a reasonable walking space around it is deductible. Measure this area. Do the same thing for every place that you permanently display your products. While none of the spaces are very large, add them up, you may be surprised. This square footage is added to any other area that is used exclusively for your business, such as an extra bedroom.

"You do not meet the test if you just put products on the table when you are conducting your Mary Kay party. The products must be permanently displayed.

FIGURING YOUR DEDUCTION

"If you have determined, with the help of your CPA, that you meet all the qualifications for a deduction, you will need to figure the percentage of your home expenses that you can deduct.

"The first thing to determine is the *Business Percentage*. To do this, compare the size of the part of your home that you use for business to your whole house. IRS says, "The following are two commonly used methods for figuring the percentage.

a. Divide the area (length multiplied by the width) used for business by the total area of your home.
b. Divide the number of rooms used for business by the total number of rooms in your home. You can use this method if the rooms in your home are all about the same size.

Example 1

- Your office is 240 square feet
- Your home is 1,200 square feet
- Your office is 20% (240/1,200) of the total area of your home
- Your business percentage is 20%

Example 2

- You use one room in your home for business
- Your home has four rooms all of about equal size
- Your office is 25% (1/4) of the total area of your home.

"Now that you know the Business Use Percentage (BUP) of your home you need to make a list of all the things you spend money on in your home. For example:

Electricity

Gas

Water

Garbage pick up

Lawn Maintenance

Maid service

Pest control

"We can go on and on, but you can see that the list, and the amount of money spent, can be substantial. For example: Your utilities (water, gas, electricity, sewer etc). add up to $250 per month, or $3,000 per year. If your BUP is 25% you can take 25% of $3,000 or $750 as a tax deduction. This will put an average of $250 extra dollars in your pocket. Just go down the list and you will be amazed at the deductions that are available.

"It doesn't matter if you own the house or rent it, you still get the deductions. Imagine being able to deduct part of the cost of scraping the barnacles off your yacht! Don't you just love it?

"Just a word of caution again, you must have a legitimate, for profit, business to qualify.

LIMIT

"Just as you are calling the barnacle scraper, I have to bring up something about limits. Yes, there are some.

IRS says, *"If your gross income from the business use of your home equals or exceeds your total business expenses (including depreciation), you can deduct all of your business expenses related to the use of your home. If your gross income from the business use is less than your total business expenses, your deduction for certain expenses for the business use of your home is limited."*

"So if your income from your business is $35,000 and the total expenses from the business use of your home is $20,000, you can take the entire $20,000 deduction.

"If the situation were reversed, your expenses were $20,000, and your total income was only $18,000, you are limited to a deduction that year of $18,000.

"What happens to the other $2,000 of expenses? You can carry those expenses over to some future tax year when you need the deduction. Then you can claim them.

"Bear in mind, we are only talking about the business use of your home, and the amount you can use to offset other income such as salary from your full time job. This has nothing to do with your mileage expense and travel and entertainment expenses, etc.

"If you have been claiming deductions for the business use of your home, there are going to be some issues when you sell the house. Be sure and consult with your CPA about the future sale of your house.

Page | 278

Chapter 15

SLAYING THE BIGGEST DRAGON OF ALL

If you are going to think. Think big.

- *Donald Trump*

"I have talked a lot about taxes and how to save money on them. Now, let's look at the Granddaddy of them all—your personal income tax.

"One of the dragons that we set out to slay was income taxes. You have seen how a home based business, even part-time, can significantly increase the jingle in your jeans. Now let's make sure the dragon stays dead. That means that we want to audit proof your business. This doesn't mean that you will never be audited. It does mean that if you are audited, you are well prepared. There is nothing to fear from an audit if you have been very careful in *documenting* (There's that word again.) all your expenses.

"First of all, having a properly constructed home based business does not increase the likelihood of an audit. Your chances of an audit are less than 2%. Don't use this figure to assume that you can get by with not correctly reporting and paying your taxes.

"Keep a couple of things in mind. First of all you have every right to be in business. Congress has mandated that the IRS assist you in your venture by allowing you to divert some of the money that would go to them, to invest in your home based business.

"Do you think that congress passed these laws because they are a bunch of great guys? Daily reading of the newspaper and watching a few news shows will prove otherwise.

"No, they had a selfish motive in providing this assistance for you. Small businesses are the largest employers in the United States. When you become successful in your business, you will either need some employees, or contract out some work to existing businesses.

"Either way, this puts the money that you diverted to your business back in the economy and increases the tax base. The goal is not to pay fewer taxes. You can zero out your taxes by just not earning any money. That's not going to work for you for very long. Your goal should be to pay the absolute minimum *percentage* of your income in taxes.

"When you are successful, you will probably pay more taxes, but the amount you pay will be a smaller percentage of your income. So congress, in some rare attack of common sense, realized that ultimately they collect more money by helping you become successful.

"Doesn't it just give you a fuzzy feeling all over, knowing these swell guys are all rooting for you? Maybe not, but we take all the breaks provided for us. It would be foolish to not take every legitimate advantage possible.

"The laws, IRS rulings, etc. that I have included to back up the strategies you have just read, are there for your benefit. The government provides them. But, the government's obligation ends there. They are not going to teach you how to take advantage of them, or tell you that you should. This is your responsibility, and now you have the tools to take advantage of them.

"People tell me all the time; 'I don't pay attention to that. My accountant takes care of it.' Your accountant doesn't take care of your taxes. Your CPA will advise you what is available, how to document the deductions, and will prepare the reports for you at the end of the year. But, it is up to you to make sure you take full advantage.

"We started the whole idea of a home based business, in order to save money on taxes, and earn more money to invest. Remember, in the example we used of the average American earning $35,000 per year? We pointed out that over their lifetime they would pay $518,000 in taxes.

"If you could save one half of these taxes, you would have $295,000 to invest. We are going to show you how to have this amount available to you in just a little while.

"Right now let's address how to make sure that you actually get to claim all these deductions.

"We have already talked about the first one. That is to document that you are going into whatever business you choose, with the intent to make a profit. The best way to do this is by preparing a business plan. This is true if you are starting a high tech business or a Network Marketing business.

"The plan doesn't have to be lengthy, but it does need to point out several things. I am going to provide you with an outline of a business plan, and instructions for completing it. You can look it over later.

"Don't panic if you have never prepared a business plan. The purpose is to bring in to focus the various opportunities and problems you will face. No business ever developed according to the original business plan. After all, you are forecasting things that will happen in the future.

"But, no matter how simple your home based business, just the act of thinking through the elements of the business plan, will increase your chances of great success.

"The documentation that you need is not nearly as cumbersome as you might imagine. You are going to have to account for your income, your expenses, and you are going to have to show proof that you paid the expenses that you claimed.

"We have mentioned several times that it is going to be absolutely necessary that you have a separate business checking account. As you deposit money in this account you need to document, in your register, where that money came from. IRS will consider every deposit as income unless you can prove that it is non-income. If you get a refund on a faulty piece of equipment you must have the documentation or it will be treated as income.

"To make sure you get all the deductions due, you need more than the cancelled check to prove expenses. You need a receipt; an invoice marked "Paid" or time sheets for employees. You need to maintain usage logs for all equipment that has a dual use.

"When your business is very small you really don't need much record keeping. Primarily your check book and receipts. It is really helpful to set up files to keep your receipts and other documents in the files. They are all in one place and orderly when it is tax time.

"At the end of each day you just drop your receipts in the appropriate file. Be sure and write the number of the check you used to pay a business expense on the receipt or invoice. This will make it a lot easier to match them up at the end of the year.

"Here are some suggestions for the labeling and use of your files.

INCOME RECORDS

In this file you should put

- Bank Statements
- Copy and explanation of all "non-income" deposits

PAYROLL RECORDS

In this file you should put

- Time sheets (Particularly if you employ family members.)
- Comparisons of what other companies pay for similar jobs

- All payroll tax forms and reports

ADVERTISING

In this file you should put

- Receipts for advertising (It's a good idea to a attach receipt to the ad.)
- Receipts for mailing costs; postage stamps, envelopes etc.
- Mail list rental

BUSINESS AUTO EXPENSE

In this file you should put

- At the end of the month, put your completed mileage logs in the file
- Auto loan interest statements
- Auto/personal property tax statement
- Record of parking and toll fees
- Record of insurance payments

LEGAL AND ACCOUNTING FEES

In this file you should put

- Receipts for legal fees
- Receipts for accounting fees including bookkeeping expenses

BUSINESS USE OF HOME

In this file you should put

- All utility bills and receipt information
- Cable bills
- Insurance bill and receipt
- Mortgage interest statement
- Bills and receipts for home improvements
- Receipts for lawn care
- Internet costs
- Receipts for payments of alarm systems charges

BUSINESS ASSETS RECORD

In this file you should put

- Receipts for all business equipment such as furniture, computer etc.
- Receipt for personal furniture converted to business use

BUSINESS EXPENSES

In this file you should put

- Invoices and receipts for office supplies
- Phone receipts
- Cell phone or pager receipts
- Stationery, fax paper etc.

"You can make a copy of these folder headings and paste them on the folders. This makes a neat way to keep track of everything.

"Be sure and keep copies of credit card bills. If you pay for business expenses of any kind by credit card, just indicate this on the bill, show the check number used to pay the bill and drop it in the file.

"Here is one more record, just to be sure. It is a good idea to keep an appointment book such as Day Timer or Franklin or a computer program and just jot down what you did for your business, even if you had no appointments on a particular day.

"This isn't a requirement, but it is a help if you ever need to prove that you have a "For Profit" intent. Of course if you have a very active business with lots of activity that is documented by long distance bills, etc. it is not a crucial point.

"Just a note saying that from 7:00 PM to 9:00 PM you were on the phone with prospects or customers is certainly proof of business activity.

"In the event you are ever audited, all the things we have talked about will be very handy, maybe crucial.

"Just a word about audits, DON'T GO! You are not required to attend an audit, and it is not a good idea. You need a tax advisor who is qualified to represent you, and depend on them. They will know what to discuss and will not make unnecessary comments that could land you in trouble.

"When I talk about being in trouble, I am not talking about legal trouble. Just that some of your deductions might be disallowed."

"Lauren, I think my brain is shutting down from trying to absorb all this information," Eric said. "There is no way I am going to remember all this stuff. I know it is important, but it is just so much."

"That's why I am here. When we put together your plan I will work with you and walk you through everything step by step. You will never use all of this, especially not all at one time.

"We will work together much like a doctor and patient. We will review all your finances, and then use what you have learned here today just as a doctor has a full pharmacopeia of treatments, we will choose the ones suited to you. This is a journey and I am available to help you all the time.

"All of you are probably feeling just as Eric does. But can you handle just one more, if it puts immediate money in your pocket?"

"I can always stand to have more jingle in my jeans," Matt said.

"Well alright then, here goes.

"How would you like an immediate increase in take home pay without working overtime or asking your boss for a raise?"

There was an immediate show of hands and Malone said, "I have been waiting on this."

"You have been learning about all the legal tax deductions that you can take on April 15. Wouldn't it be nice to take advantage of those deductions in advance? Would you fill out just one sheet of paper to qualify for the raise? "

"As long as it is just ONE sheet of paper," Allison laughed. "So tell us about this magical sheet of paper."

"When you went to work at your present job, you completed a *W-4 Employee's Withholding Allowance Certificate*. Most people think of this as relating to the exemptions you claim for your dependents.

"That is only partially true. The second page of this form is a worksheet to use in claiming allowances. The first line says, *"Use this worksheet only if you plan to itemize deductions, **claim certain credits, or claim adjustments to income on your tax return.**"*

"The perfect tax return is one where you owe no additional taxes above what has been withheld, and you have no money coming back. This form allows you to make that adjustment.

"You know you are going to owe fewer taxes because of your business deductions. So let's go ahead and start receiving the amount you usually get at the end of the year today.

"You can fill out a new W-4 form, to reflect the lower taxes, and claim additional deductions. This will increase your take home pay in your very next paycheck.

"Consult with your CPA about this, but a rule of thumb is that you can claim an additional deduction for about every $3,000 of deductible expenses.

"Let's start with your car allowance. For simplicity, assume that you are using the mileage deduction. You calculate that you are going to drive about 15,000 miles for business purposes. At $.50 per mile, your deduction is $7,500. This can put an extra $200 per month back in the pocket of the ***average*** taxpayer.

"Notice I emphasized the word ***average.*** It varies at different salary levels and number of exemptions already claimed.

"See your CPA, but here is some information to take to him. Complete this worksheet before consulting with your CPA, it will save time and expense.

BUSINESS DEDUCTON WORKSHEET

Find the BUP (Business Use Percentage) of your home.

A.   Enter total finished square feet of your home

_____

B.   Enter total square feet used in business

_____

Divide the amount on line B by amount on line A
_____%

"You can apply this percentage to each of the expense items associated with your home. Things like, mortgage or rent, utilities, trash pickup, yard work, repairs and maintenance, security systems etc.

"For example, if your BUP is 25% and yard maintenance is $100 per month, or $1,200 per year, you can claim around $300 as a tax deduction. ($1,200 X 25%).

"Apply this percentage to your utilities, your phone bill, garbage pick-up in fact to all the expenses of your home, including the rent or house payment.

"In fact some claims for a home based business have been denied by the IRS because some of these expenses weren't claimed as a deduction."

Chapter 16

THE COMPLETE SECRET SYNERGY GROUP SYSTEM

"Whatever you can do, or dream you can, begin it.
Boldness has genius, power and magic in it."

- Goethe

Lauren has unloaded a treasure trove of principles, techniques, strategies and methods on you and the protégés. Hopefully you have all of the verified all the information you have learned.

If you have been waiting to join some secret society with passwords and secret handshakes, your wait is over.

There is no formally organized society.

You become a member of the Synergy Group by just becoming one of the statistically small number of people who have ever even been exposed to this information. In the back of this book you will find information about how to expand your knowledge if you desire.

This doesn't mean I have held anything back in the book. Take the book and the knowledge you have gained, put them to use and create whatever level of wealth you can dream. You know how.

Presently there is no other book on the market that has all of the information that you have purchased. Be sure and thank whoever, or whatever, led you to this information. If you actually put it to use, they, or it, deserve your undying gratitude.

The book is written for the average person who may be struggling economically. After all, that includes most of the people alive today. However, I didn't discriminate against those of you who already have wealth or enjoy very high incomes. This information can add tremendously to that wealth or income. In this sense we are all in the same boat. You saw in the book an example of me buying $1,000,000 in one day for a friend.

I would like to bring the book to a close by reviewing exactly what comprises the Secret Synergy Group System.

The cornerstone of a financial fortress built on the Secret Synergy Group System is, of course.......

TAX LIEN CERTIFICATES

I believe that the cornerstone of the foundation should be a little, or no risk high yielding vehicle. Certainly that eliminates the stock market in any form; mutual funds included.

As long as you have your fortune anchored by an asset base that you aren't going to lose, you can pursue other investments that may even offer higher returns.

You have met several vehicles that qualify in the pages of this book. You have learned where they are, how to research them, how to buy them and how to sell them for huge profits, if you followed your training.

If you make a mistake on one of your other investments and lose some money, your future is still assured because it is anchored in a vehicle with a guaranteed *rate*.

You already know you can't just buy a Tax Lien Certificate and forget it.

- You will probably want to pay subsequent year taxes to maintain your position.

- You will want to subscribe to www.TaxSaleLists.com There is a free membership and a paid membership. If you are very active the paid membership is worth many times the cost. *I am not affiliated with this company and receive no compensation from them, though I have been a paid member for years.*

- You will want to reinvest immediately after a lien is redeemed. You must keep all your money working all the time.

- You will want to keep aware of dates to send notices if you are going to foreclose, or hire an attorney *experienced in foreclosing tax liens.*

I can't stress strongly enough that the attorney you choose must be experienced in the task at hand. The attorney that handled your cousin's divorce is probably not a good choice.

TAX DEEDS, ASSIGNMENT PURCHASES AND STRUCK OFF PROPERTIES

The next two corners can be added in whatever order you choose.

Take just one minute to review what each of these terms mean.

Tax Deeds—There are two sources of Tax Deeds.

1. States that do not sell Tax Lien Certificates take delinquent properties directly, after a period of time that varies with each state, and sell the property directly to the public. Texas and Georgia sell a Restricted Tax Deed that gives the property owner another opportunity to bring taxes current and keep the property. Other states have an absolute sale and the high bidder owns the property outright.

2. Some other states, Arizona for example, take properties that didn't sell at the Tax Lien sale and have not been redeemed and auction them. In some places, such as Arkansas and Alabama, you can buy these properties directly from the state without an auction.

In either case you are buying the property and you get a deed.

OPPORTUNITY PROPERTIES

Opportunity Properties is a term you won't hear anywhere else. As Barb and I started getting involved in this strategy we needed a short way to describe what we were doing. Barb said, "This represents a tremendous opportunity; so let's call them Opportunity Properties."

Now thousands of people know what the term means but if you ask a real estate agent, unless he is one of our subscribers, he won't have the foggiest notion.

As you have learned, this just means that you contact folks who have not been paying their real estate taxes. Offer them a token payment of $25 to $100 for their property. It is amazing how often you can buy $10,000 to $50,000, often many times more expensive chunks of real estate for tokens, and just as often for absolutely nothing.

As this is being written two of my partners and I have a $300,000 property that we have the price of two postage stamps invested. Not at all unusual.

HOME BASED BUSINESS

If you are an average American, you absolutely, positively, MUST have a home based business. I don't mean a sham business. I mean a legitimate business you run out of your home.

The tax advantages are simply too enormous to avoid this. If you need some help or ideas just email me at jimyocom@comcast.net and let me know what you need. I am happy to help. There is no additional cost to you.

The minute you PROPERLY set up your home based business you can get an immediate increase in take-home-pay by just filling out a single piece of paper.

Now, do you need all four corners set at one time? No, but you will want to explore all of them as soon as possible.

Right now you need to get started making arrangements to buy Tax Lien Certificates in a tax sheltered account such as a Roth IRA or a single 401k. We aren't even going to talk about not having enough money. Just go to www.eggmoneysavings.com and get Barb's book. You'll find all the savings you need right out of your present budget.

Here is a letter I received from someone I don't even know. But, it really sums up my feelings about working for **ME.** Perhaps you feel the same way, or you will.

"In every country in the world lies a large, industrial city. A site of one of the world's largest slave labor camps. Each morning people move **"herd-like"** from their quarters into the industrial camp. Each in his or her station by 7:00 am. Here, they report to their masters for their day's duties. They then remain there till 5:00 PM, when they are released. They have no choice on how many hours they must labor - sometimes they are required to work overtime until their master tells them they can leave.

"Each year, they are told when they can take their vacation, for how long and when they must return. They have little choice to how much money they earn. They are allowed very little time for lunch and coffee breaks during these labor hours. They remain in their chains with great fear because the masters can punish them with the **"lay-off"** whip.

"It is said that some slaves that are good and faithful have felt the sting of the whip. Day by day, year by year they toil until the master decides for them to stop working." He then releases them to the retirement camps, where they are forced to sit idle and wait for death. It's a well-known fact that old slaves that try to work are sometimes whipped with the **"stop your pension"** whip.

"I know these slave camps really exist, for I am a free man who lives among the slaves. I am in business for myself, and am truly free. I rise in the morning called for by my schedule. I decide my own hours, and of course I decide my own paycheck, because I am not a slave.

"I can choose to work when and where I please and with whom I please. I am free to stay in the city for as long as I want or to move on to the greener pastures, if I decide to.

"I have seen many slaves sadly pack their belongings, to leave the city in search for a new master. There is a ray of hope for the slave though. He or she can buy their own freedom. The cost is not high, yet it seems high to those who don't have the courage to pay the price.

"What is the price?

"One must be willing to be their own master for a truly free and successful life!"

Author: Unknown
_____

WOW!!

I know that not everyone feels they are a slave to their job. Many people have jobs they truly love. I am certainly not suggesting that you should leave your job. That is a very private and personal decision.

Our goal has been to share with you opportunities that allow you to make whatever choice is best for you.

You have in your hands all the information you need to achieve whatever level of financial success you desire. Some people learn in a different way than others. If you would like information about how receive one of our $1,500 seminars on both DVD and printed form at a discount of 80% just visit our web site: www.jimyocom.com

While you are there just noodle about for a bit. There is a ton of free information on our blog and on the different articles that we write often. If you would like to speak to one of us just call toll free, 1-866-829-9877. If we are not available at that exact moment just leave a message and we will get back to you as soon as possible. We return all calls. You can email us at jimyocom@comcast.net

You gotta do this!

Your friends in success,

Lauren, Kevin, Matt, Eric, Aaron, Dagney and Jim

Barb and Jim Yocom aka Dagney and Kevin

ABOUT THE AUTHOR

<u>JIM YOCOM</u>

- Investor/Author/Speaker
- *50 years of experience in finance and real estate*
- 1959 Field Representative – Southwestern Investment Co. Inc.
- 1962 District Manager – Allied Concord Financial Corp – Title 1 FHA and mortgage loans
- 1969 Director of Sales – Falls Land & Development Corp. – Developed a nine state sales organization for land sales and construction.
- 1973 Co-Founder and Director of Agencies – Family Home Assurance – A life insurance company 100% owned by real estate brokers

- 1979 Founder and CEO – Synergy Group Corp – A holding company for Synergy Oil Corp and Realty Elite, Inc.
- 1980 – Founder and CEO – Synergy Group, Inc. – A financial and real estate education company with 8,000 representatives in all 50 states
- 1992 Founder and CEO – Synergy Seminars, Inc. – Real estate education and investments strictly in tax defaulted properties, Tax Lien Certificates, Tax Deeds and Opportunity Properties
- 2007 – Founder and CEO – Maverick Real Estate Solutions, Inc. – Real estate investments with special emphasis on nationwide Short Sales

AUTHOR

- Set Yourself Free – A financial education program geared to real estate
- Tax Lien Certificates, *A little known government program that can make you financially independent*
- How To Beat The Pants Off The Best Wall Street Guru, *And Never Get Off Your Couch*

- The Secret Synergy Group System For Investing In Tax Lien Certificates

Far too many books and programs to list here, go to website www.jimyocom.com

APPENDIX

"The Miami Herald" article
November21, 1996

A LOST DEAL: HUZENGA LAND SOLD FOR A SONG TAX BILL BLUNDER LEADS TO AUCTION

For H. Wayne Huzenga the financial wizard who has turned struggling companies into enormous empires, this could be a $1,000,000 blunder.

But for a group of investors, it's a killer coup, at Huzenga's expense.

Broward County unloaded a million dollar chunk of land owned by a Huzenga company in northwest Broward last month at a courthouse auction—the very place where properties are sold when owners can't scrape together enough to pay their taxes.

But billionaire H. Wayne Huzenga – Owner of the Miami Dolphins and Florida Marlins – Broward County put Huzenga's Coconut Creek land on the block after one of

Huzenga's companies failed to pay a $22,000 property tax bill two years ago. Huzenga was unaware of the delinquent tax bill until after the property was sold.

"We think it's a technical oversight,' Huzenga spokesman, Stan Smith, said Wednesday. "We have a lot of property, and we didn't receive the tax bill notice."

The county sent tax bills and delinquent notices to Huzenga. His representatives say they were never received because they all went to his old address.

However it happened, four South Florida real estate investors scooped up the 10 acres during an Oct. 23 auction at the Broward County Courthouse. They paid $47,510 for the undeveloped land assessed at $700,000, and believed to be worth about $1,000,000 on the open market. The tract is part of 80 acres that Huzenga owns at the Southwest corner of Hilsboro Boulevard and Lyons Road, just south of the Palm Beach County line.

"It's right in the path of development," said one of the new owners, Bob Aebersold, a Boca Raton accountant.

eBay screen shot – Illustration 19

Here is your chance to own three, yes 3, adjoining lots in the Linn Valley Lakes private recreational facility. You are buying from the owner, not from a property dealer. We bought these lots for vacationing purposes , for us and our kids, but the kids aren't that interested and we don't think that we will use it without them. We don't really know what they are worth, but the taxes are based on $450.00 value each, so here is your chance to steal them. We are starting the bidding at enough to cover our costs and we will let you the bidder decide what the property is worth. Speaking of the property, you probably want to know what you are bidding on. We have three lots on one----- *(The rest is outside the screen shot.)*

Printed in the USA
CPSIA information can be obtained
at www.ICGtesting.com
LVHW020811070924
790421LV00010B/586

9 781482 052695